# SO YOU THINK YOU WANT TO

*The True Grit of
a Political Campaign*

# Run

# FOR CONGRESS

## GEORGE FRANKLIN

**FPA** BOOKS

# SO YOU THINK YOU WANT TO RUN FOR CONGRESS
## THE TRUE GRIT OF A POLITICAL CAMPAIGN

*FPA Books*
*7 Howell Mill Plantation*
*Atlanta, GA 30327*

*This book may be ordered through booksellers or by visiting GeorgeFranklinAuthor.com*

*The conversations in the book all come from the author's recollections, though they are not written to represent word-for-word transcripts. Rather, the author has retold them in a way that evokes the feeling and meaning of what was said and in all instances, the essence of the dialogue is accurate.*

*ISBN: 978-1-7334444-0-8 (Paperback)*
*ISBN: 978-1-7334444-1-5 (e-Book)*

*Printed in the United States of America.*

*Dedicated to every student, intern, volunteer, campaign staffer or political aficionado – Democrat, Republican, Liberal, Conservative – who ever contemplated entering the arena to make a difference.*

*A heartfelt thanks to Becky O'Dell, a special person,
who persevered with me through "Raisin Bran
and Other Cereal Wars" and now this book.
Political opposites, but soul mates.
She is the only one who can read my handwriting
and makes it all happen.*

# *Prologue*

It all began with a funeral and ended up with the political equivalent of one.

Ken Brock was a gigantic man. If you are old enough, think Burl Ives, and yes I will say the trite phrase, "He was a big man with a big heart," because it was true. He also was what you call a political operative, not someone familiar to the general public, but if you were a Democrat or Republican in Michigan politics you knew who he was. He was the guy behind the scenes in both politics and policy and when they merged, he would make things happen.

His first two loves were his wife Sue and daughter Emma followed closely by his third passion – political strategy. He loved campaigns. I guess it started with his own run for class president and student body president when he was in high school. The next 40 years, however, would be about someone else and the causes he and they believed in. Ken Brock eventually would become known as a "progressive" in the Democratic Party having once been known as a "liberal" and, before that, simply a Democrat or if you wanted to jazz it up a bit a "New Deal Democrat." I harken back to another era when I hear the current wave of Democrats talking about health care, minimum wage, right-to-work, environmental protection and workplace protection as if they are some new issues. Ken Brock fought those battles his entire adult life with the difference being he believed in the politics of the possible as opposed to the emptiness of a philosophical crusade. Ken Brock played to win. He remembered George McGovern. Ken worked in the trenches as a staff person in the Michigan House, the Michigan Senate and for a string of politicians who shared his "progressive," "liberal" and "New Deal" beliefs. Howard Wolpe, a former congressman and Michigan gubernatorial candidate; Lane Evans, a former Illinois member of Congress; Paul Simon for Senate in Illinois; Senator Bill Bradley for president; Burton Leland, a past Michigan state senator and Wayne County commissioner; Mark Schauer, past Michigan Senate minority leader, congressman and gubernatorial candidate and even the revered Dean of the Congressional Delegation, John Dingell, all benefited from Ken's counsel, guidance and political acumen.

If you are a real political junkie, you will recognize the name David Broder, who for 40 years was the chief political correspondent for *The Washington Post* and the "unofficial chairman of the board" of National Political Writers. I found it interesting as a young Hill staffer that his byline in August would often say "Beaver Island" which meant nothing to me, but as I would eventually find out is a remote location in the middle of Lake Michigan accessible only by air or boat. It was where David Broder would vacation every summer and it was also the favorite place of Ken Brock.

Not surprising that Ken would find it so attractive given its natural beauty and the opportunity to be trapped on an island with the greatest political reporter in the country whom he got to know. I always envied Ken for that.

Ken Brock died July 22, 2015, unexpectedly at the age of 55. He suffered from health issues I was not aware of. Despite his relatively young age, he made an impact on a lot of people's lives by making a difference. He incrementally made things better.

I attended his funeral July 31 in East Lansing, Michigan and, as you might expect, it was crowded with a cadre of Democratic Party officials and activists. What I didn't expect was that Zack Pohl, a former Mark Schauer aide and the spokesman for the AFL-CIO, would read Ken's favorite quote which ironically was from a Republican named Teddy Roosevelt:

*"It is not the critic who counts; not the man who points out how the strong man stumbles, or where the doer of deeds could have done them better. The credit belongs to the man who is actually in the arena, whose face is marred by dust and sweat and blood; who strives valiantly; who errs, who comes short again and again, because there is no effort without error and shortcoming; but who does actually strive to do the deeds; who knows great enthusiasms, the great devotions; who spends himself in a worthy cause; who at the best knows in the end the triumph of high achievement, and who at the worst, if he fails, at least fails*

*while daring greatly, so that his place shall never be with those cold and timid souls who neither know victory nor defeat."*

Maybe I should be embarrassed to admit that I was not familiar with this most famous quote of Teddy Roosevelt. Suffice it to say, it had an impact on me and others gathered at River Terrace Church for Ken's parting service. I thought about it the entire hour and a half ride back to Kalamazoo. I really thought about it on Wednesday, November 9, fifteen months later.

*"The problem with political jokes is that they get elected."*
**Henry Cate**

## Chapter 1

"My God, what have we done?" was my response to my wife Molly, as we watched Hillary Clinton concede to President-elect Donald Trump on the morning of November 9, 2016. Just moments before Hillary walked out to speak, I saw my good friend Jim Margolis take a seat in the second row. Jim had been her media advisor having served in that same capacity in both of President Obama's campaigns. He looked totally spent. I would find out later when we finally had a chance to talk that uncharacteristically, he was sure they were going to win this one. In other campaigns, he was always the glass is half empty guy. This time he thought the glass was full. What had happened?

A major portion of the so called "blue wall" had collapsed. The blue wall was comprised of states that were supposedly a lock for Democrats in presidential contests. Somehow the unthinkable had happened. Pennsylvania, Michigan and Wisconsin had all gone for Trump, albeit by narrow margins, but the margin was meaningless, since the Electoral College does not factor in the spread. Winner takes all. (Ever since that election night, I have said you have to give the devil his due. Literally, the last stop of the last night of the Trump campaign was Grand Rapids, Michigan sometime after midnight. Donald Trump won Michigan by 10,704 votes or .3%, which is a number of votes you might expect to win a state House seat, not a presidential race from a state with 10 million people. Last stop; last night. They knew exactly what they were doing).

How Trump won did not matter. He won. We had elected a real life version of Richie Rich, the comic book character, but devoid of any positive attributes of young Mr. Rich. Daddy had given Donald everything, including his draft deferment. Donald Trump was a charlatan who was morally vacuous, politically unprincipled and lacked any core philosophical beliefs other than self-aggrandizement to guide him when he took office. Mitt Romney, former Republican presidential nominee, called it the way it was in a blistering speech in March 2016 before the election. Romney described Donald Trump as a "fraud," evaluated his promises as "worthless" and went on to claim, "He's playing the American people for suckers." Senator John McCain, another Republican presidential nominee chimed in with a statement declaring, "I share the concerns about Donald Trump that my friend and former Republican nominee Mitt Romney described." What they said on March 2016 was true then and still true on November 9, the day after the election. Now what do we do about it?

I have been in and around Democratic politics for my entire adult life, starting with working for Congressman Frank Thompson (D-NJ) while in college and law school. A period which included campaign work for George McGovern, traveling to Arizona to help Roberto Reveles, the first significant Mexican American candidate for Congress in that state and finally a stint in the Florida Legislature, which was a real eye opener into the wild and wooly world of state law making. Once out of law school, I was an Election Day counsel in the Carter presidential campaign, served on an Agriculture Advisory Board in the Carter administration and then as a Trade Advisory Board Member in the Clinton administration. After moving to Michigan with Kellogg Company in 1987, I was appointed to the Western Michigan University Board of Trustees by Governor Jim Blanchard where I served for 11 years and was then appointed to the State Officers Compensation Commission by Governor Granholm.

As I said, a lot of in and around Democratic politics, but with one major glaring omission. I had never been a candidate for office. Maybe it was time to consider entering the arena with a run for Congress.

If you are considering upending your life, your family and everybody around you for the next couple of years, it might be wise to analyze the organization you are attempting to join. In other words, what is Congress and who are these solons who make up the House of Representatives?

Now before delving too deeply into the history and composition of Congress, it might also be wise to consider the admonition of Mark Twain who reportedly exhorted that, "There is no distinctly native American criminal class, except Congress." His denunciation of Congress might also make you want to consider the sage counsel of Groucho Marx who proclaimed he didn't, "want to belong to any club that will have me as a member." Two cautionary statements that should make you think twice about leaping into the political fray.

———————

Many voters, when you say Congress, think of the House of Representatives separate from the Senate. In fact, both bodies constitute Congress as created in the Constitution in Article I, Section 1.

### Section 1

*"All legislative powers herein granted shall be vested in a Congress of the United States, which shall consist of a Senate and House of Representatives."*

The Constitution goes on in the next section to describe qualifications required to become a member of the House of Representatives.

### Section 2

*"The House of Representatives shall be composed of members chosen every second year by the people of the several states, and electors in each state shall have the qualifications requisite for the most numerous branch of the state legislature.*

*No person shall be a be a representative who shall not have attained to the age of twenty-five years, and been seven years a citizen of the United States, and who shall not, when elected, be an inhabitant of that state in which he shall be chosen."*

———————

In a nutshell, the requirements for becoming a member of a rather exclusive club – the House of Representatives, are rather minimal. You must be 25-years-old, a U.S. citizen for at least seven years and a resident of the state. You don't even need to live in the district from which you are running. Maybe Groucho was right.

The Congress, when Donald Trump took office in January of 2017, was numerically the 115th Congress, which is somewhat misleading since it fails to account for numerous "Congresses" before the "first" in March of 1789. It does not take into account the First Continental Congress in September of 1775 comprised of 55 men (yes, all male and all white) that met for seven weeks and whipped together a document called the Declaration of Independence which, along with others, was boldly signed by John Hancock, so that King George could read his name without his spectacles. Not a bad piece of work for the first Congress.

The First Continental Congress was followed in May of 1775 by the Second Continental Congress and was comprised of representatives of all 13 colonies, resulting in the creation of the Articles of Confederation. Upon final approval by the colonies in 1781, the articles established a Congress who in turn elected John Hanson as the first president of the United States in Congress Assembled. Considering the title, was George Washington really the first president? There would be eight Congresses under the articles, but after six, the member states started to realize that the articles had not been such a good idea after all. So in May of 1787, the 55 men met again in Philadelphia to form the Constitutional Convention and put together the U.S. Constitution or as some historians refer to it, a "bundle of compromises." It was a political battle of wills between the Federalists and the anti-Federalists which vaguely brings to mind Democrats vs. Republicans and how things never seem to change. Finally, on June 21, 1788, New Hampshire became the ninth state to ratify the new document called the Constitution of the United States of America and it was agreed that this new government with its first Congress would convene March 4, 1789, with 65 members. One of their first acts was to propose 12 amendments to the Constitution, 10 of which were ratified, becoming what we now call the Bill of Rights.

Since that august initial meeting in 1789 and beginning with the 115th Congress and the Trump administration 228 years later in January of 2017, 10,946 individuals had served in the House of Representatives. Rather rarefied air if you consider the length of time and that we are now a nation of approximately 330,000,000 people.

The House of Representatives in 2017 looked very different from the first group gathered in 1789. It consisted of 435 members (excluding five delegates and the commissioner from Puerto Rico) of which 241 identified as Republicans and 194 Democrats. Eighty-four members were women – 62 were Democrats and 22 were Republicans. The average age was 57.8-years-old with the youngest being 32-year-old Elise Stefanik (R-NY) and the oldest 87-year-old John Conyers (D-MI).

| | |
|---|---|
| 241 or 55.4% | Protestant |
| 141 or 32.4% | Catholic |
| 22 or 5.0% | Jewish |
| 7 | Mormon |

| | |
|---|---|
| 3 | Hindu |
| 2 | Muslim |
| 2 | Buddhist |

Other religious affiliations represented include Pentecostal Christian, Unitarian Universalist, Greek Orthodox, and Christian Science religions.

The House was also comprised of 48 African Americans (46 Democrats, 2 Republicans) and 2 Native Americans or Indigenous, both of whom were Republican. Looking back at the Constitutional Convention as a "bundle of compromises" and considering the diversity of modern day legislative bodies, anyone running for office better be prepared to drop the "my way or the highway" approach to campaigning. It just isn't going to happen.

By running for a seat in the House of Representatives, you are asking voters to make you one four hundred thirty-fifth, of one-half, of one-third of the United States government. I looked at the composition of the Congress I hoped to join the next time around and took note that while older than average, I would not be the oldest by any means. I also saw a large contingent of Catholics and, as a kid who grew up in the South Side of Chicago, I would not be the only one who understood the most terrifying sight was a nun with a ruler. In addition, my training as a lawyer and a member of the bar might come in handy drafting and interpreting statutes in a body with more than 160 members with a Juris Doctor degree. Finally, I thought as someone who had held a "real job" as a corporate officer of Kellogg Company and a small business man, I might have some perspectives to lend to my fellow members in the Democratic caucus.

It is a big leap from thinking about running for political office to actually doing it. It entails hours of soul searching about your own commitment and motivations for such an undertaking. It also requires time spent with those close to you and honestly listening to their take on what you are considering.

Lastly, you need to factor in the political realities. In my case, after evaluating all of the aforementioned aspects, it was becoming apparent to me that Teddy Roosevelt was about to call my bluff.

*"Instead of giving a politician the keys to the city, it might be better to change the locks."*
**Doug Larson**

# Chapter 2

The Village of Colon is the official "Magic Capital of the World." It is the former home and burial site of the famous Harry Blackstone, "The Great Blackstone," one of the most notable illusionists and magicians of the 20th century. It is also the headquarters of The Abbott Magic Company, FAB Magic Company and Sterlini Magic Manufacturing Company, all businesses that make supplies and tricks for budding and established prestidigitators and tricksters around the world.

Glenn, where the main intersection is a blinking light, is known as the "Pancake Town." Local lore has it that on December 7, 1937, more than 200 motorists found themselves stranded in a snowstorm in this tiny town where they were forced to seek shelter. Dwindling supplies necessitated reliance on pancakes for breakfast, lunch and dinner for the entire community. You can argue the details, but it's great marketing ammunition to entice those summer tourists with a piece of Americana.

Yes, there really is a Kalamazoo. A funny name derived from the local Potawatomi Indians meaning "bubbling water" or the more cosmic "the mirage of reflecting river." Truth is, no one is quite sure what it really means, but the name is quirky enough to warrant the attention of the Glenn Miller Band in 1942 to create the number one hit in the land, *"I've Got a Gal in Kalamazoo."* Part college town, part rustbelt, home of the first outdoor pedestrian mall and big enough to have at least one of everything you need without big city hassles and with genuine Midwest values.

Colon, Glenn and Kalamazoo have one political common denominator. They are all part of the 6th Congressional District of Michigan. A "lean Republican" district (according to *The Cook Political Report* a R+4), six counties (all but a tiny sliver of one), held by Republican Fred Upton since he took office in 1987. The district encompasses the southwest corner of Michigan and its population of 705,974, according to the 2010 Census is:

| | |
|---|---|
| 82.2% | White |
| 8.4% | Black |
| 5.3% | Hispanic |
| 1.3% | Asian |
| .5% | Native American |

Largely a rural district, here farmers grow corn, soybeans and specialty crops (fancy name for fruits and vegetables). It is also headquarters for Whirlpool and Stryker, includes a major presence of Perrigo, Pfizer and a large contingent of Kellogg Company employees. Academic institutions include Western Michigan University, Kalamazoo College as well as numerous community colleges. It has a diversified economy, including tourism, based in large part on its extensive Lake Michigan shoreline.

Politically, Michigan's 6th Congressional District is the swing part of a swing state. In 2017, Republicans controlled all branches of government in the capital of Lansing, but historically that has not always been the case. Looking at the past few presidential elections in the 6th will give you a feel for its political volatility:

| 2016 | Trump | 51% – 43% |
| 2012 | Romney | 50% – 49% |
| 2008 | Obama | 54% – 45% |
| 2004 | Bush | 53% – 46% |
| 2000 | Bush | 52% – 45% |
| 1996 | Clinton | 46% – 44% |
| 1992 | Clinton | 39% – 38%. |

That makes it 4 Republicans to 3 Democrats in the presidential contests since the 1990's. Remember, a lean Republican district.

The congressional seat over this same period tells quite a different story. (I have omitted third party votes, which peaked at 5% in 2016):

| 2016 | Upton | 58% – 36% |
| 2014 | Upton | 56% – 40% |
| 2012 | Upton | 55% – 43% |
| 2010 | Upton | 62% – 34% |
| 2008 | Upton | 59% – 39% |
| 2006 | Upton | 61% – 38% |
| 2004 | Upton | 65% – 32% |
| 2002 | Upton | 69% – 29% |

| 2000 | Upton | 68% – 29% |
| 1998 | Upton | 70% – 28% |
| 1996 | Upton | 68% – 31% |
| 1994 | Upton | 73% – 26% |
| 1992 | Upton | 62% – 38%. |

It doesn't take a Ph.D. in political science to figure out that the incumbent Fred Upton is very popular. Even when the Democratic presidential candidate was carrying the district in 1992, 1996 and 2008, Fred won the district 62% – 38%, 68% – 31% and 59% – 39%.

*6th Congressional District Map*

A quick overview of the six counties that make up the 6th District will give you a political feel for the territory and the politics of the region.

From the northwest going counter-clockwise is:

Allegan County, the county in which a sliver is part of another congressional district – namely the 2nd Congressional District, includes the city of Holland from the northern tip of the county. The bulk of the county belongs in the 6th Congressional District and is primarily rural, including extensive portions of the Lake Michigan shoreline with the resort towns of Saugatuck and Douglas. The population of Allegan is at last count 111,403 spread out over 1,833 square miles for a density of 135 per sq. mi. and consists of:

| | |
|---|---|
| 92.9% | Caucasian |
| 6.2% | Hispanic |
| 1.2% | African American |
| .6% | Asian |
| .6% | Native American |

The politics in Allegan are very red. Trump beat Clinton 60.9% to 32.2% in 2016 with third parties securing 6.9% of the total. The last time a Democratic presidential candidate won the county was in 1964 when Johnson squeaked by Goldwater 51.5% to 48.4%.

South of Allegan County and hugging the Lake Michigan coast is:

Van Buren County, named for Martin Van Buren during his tenure as secretary of state before becoming president. It is one of Michigan's so called "Cabinet counties," of which there were 10 named after members of President Andrew Jackson's Cabinet. The 76,353 residents hold a little more hope for the Democrats, but it is still a tough slog. Largely rural, with a density of 156 per sq. mi., tourism has a major impact on the economy with the largest city being the port town of South Haven where the annual Blueberry Festival is held in homage to proliferation of blueberry farms in the area. The interior of the county is dotted with inland lakes and numerous second homes. Trump won the county 53.8% vs. Hillary with 39.8% and third parties collectively at 6.4%. Interestingly, Obama won Van Buren in 2008 53.5% to 44.7% and again in 2012 (barely) 49.6% to 49.2%. Some hope for Democrats.

Continuing south along Lake Michigan's shoreline to the Indiana border is:

Berrien County, considered the heart of the fruit belt in Michigan, with a population of 156,813. Also unknown to many, Berrien County was the longtime home of world champion boxer Muhammad Ali who called his 81-acre estate Rope-A-Dope. It is a county which has favored the Republican presidential ticket in all but six elections since 1884. The one bright spot for Democrats is that in 2018 Obama actually carried the county in 2008 with 51.9%, but then lost it in 2012 by only 52.5% to 46%. Trump won Berrien with

53.7% to Hillary with 41% and 5.4% going third party. The one ray of hope for Democrats in Berrien County and the somewhat eternal question is whether the abysmal voter turnout in largely the African American Benton Harbor can be improved. Literally, across the river from Benton Harbor is the toney beach community of St. Joseph which is the home of the incumbent Congressman Fred Upton. His family founded Whirlpool and one of the main drags in town is named Upton Street after his family.

Moving inland (east) along the Indiana border is:

Cass County, the least populated (52,293) county and the least dense at 105 per sq. mi. which was an important factor in the Underground Railroad. Quakers who lived in Cass would protect fleeing slaves from the South, resulting in Kentucky slaveholders raiding the county only to be met with "angry farmers armed with clubs, scythes and other farm instruments" resisting their assaults. Today the county is very red. Trump trounced Hillary 63% to 32.2%. Obama did eke out a win in 2008 51.3% to 47.1%, but then got walloped in 2012 56.3% to 42.7%. All in all, a rather bleak picture for Democrats.

The next county east along the Indiana border is:

St. Joseph County with a reliably "red" population of 61,295, is home to a major Monsanto seed corn operation in the heart of farm country with a density of only 122 per sq. mi. This Republican stronghold has gone with the Republican Party presidential nominee 79% of the elections (27 of 34) since 1884. Trump won St. Joseph 62.1% to Hillary's 31.4% with 6.5% going third party. The last time a Democratic candidate for president won St. Joseph was the Johnson landslide of 1964. This neck of the woods is very tough sledding for any Democrat.

Due north of St. Joseph is the most populous county in the 6th Congressional District:

Kalamazoo, whose county seat is the city of Kalamazoo, is affectionately referred to by the Democrats as the "blue bubble." This county also includes the city of Portage which grew rapidly in the 60's and 70's arguably as a result of white flight from school integration and deteriorating race relations. The county is:

| | |
|---|---|
| 80.1% | Caucasian |
| 11.1% | African American |
| 4.0% | Hispanic |
| 2.2% | Asian |
| .5% | Native American |

Home to Kalamazoo College, Western Michigan University, and more than 8,000 students at Kalamazoo Valley Community College, it is a mix of Democrat and Republican office holders. The prosecutor and sheriff are both Democrats as is the drain commissioner. The 11-member board of county commissioners in 2017 was controlled six to five by Democrats. The county has gone for the Democratic presidential ticket since 1992, with Trump losing to Hillary Clinton 53.2% to 40.4% in 2016.

To recap:

| County | Population | Politics |
|--------|-----------|----------|
| Cass | 52,293 | Red |
| St. Joseph | 61,295 | Red |
| Van Buren | 71,353 | Pink |
| Allegan | 111,403 | Red |
| Berrien | 156,813 | Red |
| Kalamazoo | 261,254 | Blue |

Once again, you don't need to have an advanced degree in statistics or political science to figure out the winning strategy for a Democrat. Win and win big in Kalamazoo and then hang on by not losing too big in the other five counties.

*"Take a good look at me,
because you'll never recognize me once
my opponent gets done with me."*
**Leonard Boswell, Iowa Congressman**

# Chapter 3

"At long last, have you left no sense of decency?" implored Joseph Welch, chief counsel for the U.S. Army, to Senator Joseph McCarthy during the Army-McCarthy hearings on June 9, 1954. The McCarthy hearings were possibly the apex of the politics of personal destruction. Regretfully, this modus operandi is common practice in political campaigns where "directors of research" implement "oppo research" through "trackers," "push polls," "whispering campaigns" and negative advertising. Dirty, vicious and mean spirited are some of the adjectives to describe this brand of politics – with just one more – effective.

Most current political observers will remember President Bill Clinton calling for an end to the politics of personal destruction in regard to his relationship with White House intern Monica Lewinsky. This was not the first time this term would be used. It actually dates back a couple of hundred years to June 3, 1808, when Massachusetts Governor James Sullivan wrote to Thomas Jefferson that the "principal object" of the Federalist appeared to be "the political and even the personal, destruction of John Quincy Adams." An effort which failed miserably considering John Quincy Adams became president in 1825. The failure of this approach, however, was insufficient to halt the practice of negative campaigning. It was only the beginning.

As Lee Atwater, the now deceased Republican strategist used to say, "If you want to know what the American people are thinking, listen to country music and watch wrestling." He was an astute observer and architect of the American political scene. He learned his craft working for Senator Strom Thurmond and Congressman Carroll Campbell, who later became governor of South Carolina. Meaner than a snake, his brutal tactics became legendary, much of which he publicly regretted on his deathbed.

Remember Willie Horton? If so, it's because of Lee Atwater. Horton was an African American who was convicted of murder and given a life sentence. Subsequently, while Michael Dukakis was the governor of Massachusetts, Horton was given a weekend furlough during which he raped a woman, pistol whipped her fiancé and stole his car. He was eventually apprehended and given two consecutive life terms to ensure as the judge said, "He would never draw a breath of fresh air again."

"While I didn't invent negative politics, I am one of the most ardent practitioners," declared Lee Atwater, and he proved it with Willie Horton in 1988. Advising Republican presidential candidate George H. W. Bush, Atwater declared (in reference to Democratic opponent Michael Dukakis) that, "He would strip the bark off that little bastard and make Willie Horton his running mate." He succeeded in doing both. He created a soft on crime ad featuring Horton that carried significant racial overtones while laying the blame for the weekend pass mayhem squarely in the lap of Michael Dukakis. Ugly, nasty, and effective. George H. W. Bush trounced Dukakis.

Lee Atwater is also credited with instituting "push polls" that would result in "whispering campaigns," possibly the most famous of which was implemented by his protégé, Karl Rove, in the South Carolina presidential Republican primary. In 2000, Senator John McCain had beaten Governor George W. Bush in the New Hampshire primary and seemed headed to victory in military friendly South Carolina. All of a sudden an anonymous poll asked South Carolina voters, "Would you be more or less likely to vote for John McCain if you knew he had fathered a black child out of wedlock?"

Not slander since it was a question, but meant to push you away from McCain and start people "whispering." It just so happened that Senator McCain and wife Cindi had adopted a dark skinned daughter from Bangladesh and pictures of his family helped "prove" what people were talking about in coffee shops and diners throughout the state. Vicious, underhanded, morally bankrupt, but effective. George W. Bush won the South Carolina primary and went on to become president of the United States.

Although both Lee Atwater and Karl Rove happen to be Republican, this is not meant to imply they corner the market on negative campaigning. Quite the contrary. Democrats have a long history of unsavory political activities to match. Franklin Delano Roosevelt instructed an aide to disseminate a rumor that the Republican nominee for president, Wendell Wilkie, had an extramarital affair with the instruction that, "We can't have any of our principal speakers refer to it, but people down the line can get it out."

President Lyndon Baines Johnson reportedly had the FBI monitor Robert Kennedy and also install a wiretap on Senator Barry Goldwater. It is also alleged that President Obama had a "research director" from the Democratic National Committee (DNC) appointed to a similar position in the legal departments of the White House for a month or so when first elected so that the individual would have access to the files of former President George W. Bush. The individual then returned to the DNC with a mother lode of information on the Republicans.

"Trackers" are everywhere. What is a "tracker?" Simply put, they are individuals who film and/or tape primary and general election candidates hoping to catch what are often called a "macaca moment." A "macaca" moment refers to an incident in which Senator George Allen (R-VA), while running against James Webb, referred to his opponent's tracker as a macaca, a Portugese word for monkey. The tracker, it so happens, was of Indian descent and great umbrage was taken over what was perceived to be a racial slight. The tape of Senator Allen calling him a macaca became a staple of the campaign and is generally attributed as a major reason he lost the election. Lost in all the clamor was the question of whether having someone pounce with every human foible is healthy. I remember snickering with Senator Debbie Stabenow, who was up for re-election in 2018, over the fact that the Republicans had a tracker filming her everywhere, even while she was buying a Christmas knick-knack gift in Frankenmuth, Michigan. It got to the point where she knew most trackers on a first name basis.

During the primary campaign, we would routinely spot a Republican tracker at forums and other public events. They would have, no kidding, spy like equipment to film and tape us. Fair I guess, but rather dispiriting. Sadly, one Democratic opponent would use college kids to surreptitiously tape me looking to catch that macaca moment. Guess they were trying to instill in them the Lee Atwater/Karl Rove values for the next generation of Democratic strategists.

Next time you see someone identified as director of research for a political campaign, remember the activities are not as mundane as the title might suggest. More than likely, the portfolio will include, in addition to issue positions and related activities, "trackers," "push polls," "whispering campaigns," negative phone banks and advertising as part of all the seamy aspects of "oppo research."

*"Politics is the art of looking for trouble, finding it everywhere, diagnosing it incorrectly and applying the wrong remedy."*
**Groucho Marx**

# Chapter 4

If you seriously consider running for Congress, the first thing you need to do is look in the mirror. Not the one you look at every day, but one of those lighted make-up mirrors you find in hotels that show you what you don't want to see. Think of Roy Moore, Al Franken, Anthony Weiner, not to mention Brett Kavanaugh who had his actions in high school come back to haunt him. You are about to undergo the political equivalent of a colonoscopy whether you have been prepped or not, so you might as well get ready.

The election of Donald J. Trump jarred me into considering something I had never really seriously contemplated before. Running for Congress. Appreciating the magnitude of this leap, I thought maybe I should start by talking with someone who had actually been a candidate in a big time campaign and who I could trust. I called Mark Schauer in early December 2017 and told him lunch was on me. Mark is an old guard liberal labor Democrat and a warrior for all the causes those labels entail. Indicative of his commitment, a few months before announcing he was running for governor of Michigan, he was pepper sprayed by police outside the state Capitol in Lansing where some 12,000 Democratic Party and labor activists were demonstrating in a show of force against the proposed right-to-work legislation. Mark had worked his way up the political ladder the conventional way. He was elected Battle Creek city commissioner, state representative and state senator where he became the minority leader. He was also a one-term member of Congress where he was given the bum's rush after voting for The Affordable Care Act (Obamacare) and finally he ran as the Democratic nominee for governor in 2014, losing narrowly to the incumbent Governor Rick Snyder. He is a battle tested guy who knew how to win and what it was like to lose. Just the person I needed to talk with.

We were both wrong from the get go on the most fundamentally important assessment of the race. Sitting down for lunch after the normal chit-chat, we quickly got into what a travesty the Trump election was and would become. I told Mark that after lecturing my daughters for years about being involved and making a difference, maybe it was time for me to leave the sidelines and enter the fray. I also referenced Ken Brock's funeral and the impact it had on me. Ken had worked for Mark. Maybe it was time for me to enter the arena.

As I mentioned, we were very wrong in the most critical factor, which was whether the incumbent Republican officeholder Fred Upton would run again. We both assumed he would not. Fred had been chair of the Energy and Commerce Committee, but was term-limited in that capacity by House Republican Caucus rules. Upton had no connection with Trump and, in fact, had refused to endorse him even after the primaries and the Republican Convention and called his refusal to endorse his intent to "stay in his own lane." The prevailing wisdom was that Fred, a 32-year incumbent, would hang it up or launch a campaign for the U.S. Senate. Eleven months later on November 17, 2017, we would find out how wrong we and the prevailing wisdom would turn out to be.

Everybody entering a political campaign is going to have some baggage to contend with unless you come directly from a monastery. You can't live 30, 40, 50, 60 (in my case – 66) years without having "stuff" you did or did not do and if you are under 30, you will be attacked for inexperience. Simply put, you will get attacked. Sad, but true.

In my case, there were some obvious hits I would take along with unanticipated shots later down the pike. I had been a corporate lawyer, lobbyist who had supported Fred Upton. *Corporate, lawyer, lobbyist and Fred Upton.* Five dirty words to the new wave of progressive Democrats. Mark and I recognized the travails those characterizations would present, but I, possibly naively, planned to run right at them. I was very proud of having been a corporate officer of Kellogg Company, a company whose profits in large part funded the W.K. Kellogg Foundation, one of the greatest philanthropic institutions in the world. I was proud to have had my own successful company, Franklin Public Affairs, LLC, where I was an advocate for cancer research at the University of Michigan, economic development in the city of Battle Creek and enhanced food safety in the nation by securing funding for The International Food Protection Training Institute created by the W.K. Kellogg Foundation. As far as my contributions to Fred Upton and other Republicans, it was part of being an advocate for my clients and their causes. (Particularly galling was that my principal attacker in the primary had lobbyists doing the exact same thing on his behalf to secure the diabetes programs he touted, but somehow that was different. More on that later).

Sure, I was the corporate lawyer/lobbyist who had supported Fred Upton and other Republicans, but looking ahead there didn't seem to be anyone on the horizon with any Washington or legislative experience with the exception of Representative Jon Hoadley who had indicated no interest in running. (Two other elected officials, Kalamazoo Prosecutor Jeff Getting and Kalamazoo Sheriff Richard Fuller, both highly respected would have been formidable candidates, but they likewise did not seem inclined to run). I also had national connections and a history of involvement in the Democratic Party that would provide support and funding in both the primary and general elections.

One other aspect of my encouraging lunch with Mark was a discussion of how to reassemble some of his campaign team for my effort. Mark was now professionally affiliated with some of his past consultants and they were a ready-made outfit with experience and with whom I would be comfortable. It would also keep Mark involved and energized since he would have a stake in the race and his imprimatur and connections would be a huge plus for me in a Democratic primary where activists would be challenging my bona fides considering my business/lobbyist background. It also helped that the lead partner at the media company, Prism Communications, would be B.J. Neidhardt who while somewhat inscrutable and always blunt was someone I respected and enjoyed. (I always got a kick out of his tough guy image. B.J. was a real softy when his little daughter was involved.) Prism was a big time media company with the normal mix of wins and losses. Nobody wins them all. Reminds me of a sailing coach who used to say, "If you meet a sailor who has never run aground, they are either a liar or not a sailor."

If I ran, I would do it with the Schauer team.

A campaign for political office is guaranteed to be disruptive, intrusive and sometimes painful. You better have your family on board and be ready for the ride. In my case, it was not a tough sell to my wife even though she knew exactly what "we" were getting into. My two daughters from a previous marriage were grown and living in Chicago and Los Angeles. Christy was married with two small children and Katy was pursuing a writing career in Chicago. As such, they were removed from any day-to-day impact of campaigning. Katy and Christy were supportive, but it was Molly, my wife, who would have to endure the craziness and the brickbats of the campaign. Fortunately, she had spent most of her professional life in politics last having served as the chief of staff to the late Senator Paul Coverdell (R) of Georgia. She knew what political life and campaigns were all about. So that December 2017, after the lunch with Mark, she and I talked about my potentially running for Congress. I expressed my concern over Trump and my interest and willingness to put myself out there to try and make a difference. She was, as with most things, totally supportive. "If you want to do it, go for it," she said. If she had stomped her foot and said, "Hell no," I wouldn't be writing this book now, but by her indulgence she had called my hand. I found myself seriously considering running for Congress.

*"Since a politician never believes what he says, he is quite surprised to be taken at his word."*
**Charles de Gaulle**

# *Chapter* 5

"Are you nuts?" "Are you crazy?" "Are you out of your f---ing mind?" Some variations of these were the usual reaction of friends and family when I mentioned I was considering running for Congress. It begs the fundamental question of every potential candidate. Why am I doing this? It is imperative to try and answer this question honestly since you will ask yourself again and again during the process just why the hell am I doing this.

I didn't need a job. I didn't need the money. Most of our friends were either contemplating retirement, getting retired or were retired. I had met and interacted with an untold number of presidents, governors, senators and members of Congress, so the celebrity aspect of political office had faded long ago. Looking back on it maybe I was "nuts, "crazy" or out of my "f---ing mind," because despite all the aforementioned reasons not to run I thought maybe I could actually go and make a difference. If I was fortunate enough to win, the day after the election, I would not be obsessed with getting re-elected with all the fundraising and kowtowing that it would require. I could vote my conscience like my friend Mark Schauer did when getting ready to vote for The Affordable Care Act (Obamacare). The day of the vote, he looked back at his chief of staff and said, "I am going across the street to lose my House seat, but it is the right thing to do." A prophetic, but a very classy declaration, because that is exactly what happened. To his credit, he never regretted voting his conscience.

I sincerely believe that deep down all people want is a fair shot at getting ahead and this was the core of my campaign and the mantra of my stump speech. It was derived from an incident during my college days and a lifetime of seeing first-hand how the system is skewed to those with wealth and access. Look at how we fund football stadiums for billionaires, but can't find the money to build new schools.

The incident to which I refer occurred during the congressional summer recess of 1971 in room B353 in the Rayburn House Office Building where I was alone manning the office of the Special Subcommittee on Labor of the Committee on Education and Labor chaired by my boss Congressman Frank Thompson (D-NJ). In walked a blue collar looking guy who asked, "Is this the Special Subcommittee on Labor?" To which I responded, "Yes." He then simply and straightforwardly asked me, "Can you help me get a job?" I was dumbfounded by his question and had no answer. This was a place of national policy, programs, initiatives and all that other highfalutin BS you hear spewed out of D.C. Get you a job? What the hell kind of question was that? After hemming and hawing for a minute or two, I explained that he would have to go to the District of Columbia Employment Office and blah, blah, blah. He responded with a blank stare and commented as he left, "Okay, I thought that was what you were here to do."

I have no idea who he was, where he went or what became of him, but I will never forget him. He didn't ask for a special favor, amendment or provision. He didn't want to be put in front of the queue or given an advantage over someone else. He simply wanted a job or as I liked to put it, a fair shot. It struck me the moment he left, isn't that really what we are here to do and that has stuck with me ever since. It reminds me of former Michigan legislator Ed LaForge, who used to like to step outside the House chambers into the gaggle of lobbyists gathered and somewhat tongue and cheek yell out, "Who is the lobbyist for the poor people out here?" I had been the lobbyist for Kellogg Company. Philip Morris, Exxon and Boeing all had lobbyists as did Planned Parenthood, the YMCA, the League of Conservation Voters and the UAW. It seems like everybody has a lobbyist, except for that guy walking in and looking for a job. In the fall of 2017, I thought to myself why don't I become his lobbyist and do it from the inside as a member of Congress.

Sometimes an innocuous or even funny moment can impact you in ways you would never imagine. Dr. Joe Schwarz, was a licensed medical doctor and practicing physician who simultaneously pursued a political career – Mayor of Battle Creek, state senator, Republican primary candidate for governor and a one-term member of Congress. His success and failures in the political world stemmed from his penchant to be blunt and not suffer fools lightly. As the Republican Party took a more rightward tilt, Schwarz stayed the moderate course.

In 2004, Joe ran in the Republican primary for the open 7th Congressional District of Michigan. In the contest, in addition to Joe, were five hard core conservatives who managed to split the right wing vote and thereby allowing him to win the nomination with 28% of the vote. He went on to win the general election in that staunch Republican district 58% to 36%.

The 2006 Republican primary was quite a different story. One of the 2004 primary opponents, Tim Walberg, decided to take another run and this time it was Walberg, the evangelical arch conservative one on one with Joe, the moderate. By consolidating the conservative vote, Walberg prevailed 53% to 47% and went on to win the general election in November. No love lost between those two.

What all this had to do with me running for Congress years later manifested itself in two aspects. While Schwarz and Walberg were pummeling each other in the 2006 Republican primary, I was minding my own business driving along Oakland Boulevard in Kalamazoo when the phone rang. It was Congressman John Dingell (D-MI) the Dean of the Michigan Delegation and without question the most powerful and influential member of Congress of our state. I almost drove off the road. What came next surprised me even more. He wanted me to run for Congress as a Democrat in the 7th Congressional District, to which I responded that might be difficult for a couple of reasons. First, I was supporting Joe Schwarz, to which he replied he was also. He went on to explain that they were concerned that Joe would not survive the primary and that the Democrats would not have a viable candidate to take on Walberg in the general election. It was somewhat Machiavellian, but intriguing. Secondly, I did not live in the 7th Congressional District, which was not a legal requirement, but as a practical matter important. I assume they thought my position at Kellogg and my activities in Battle Creek would compensate for my being a non-resident.

It was all going to be too complicated and I told Congressman Dingell such. In addition, for personal reasons, the time was not right to take on such an undertaking. Quite a compliment being asked, but it was a no go.

One spinoff of the Schwarz-Walberg encounter had a humorous aspect which also impacted me later in deciding to run for Congress. As I mentioned there was no love lost between Schwarz and Walberg, and payback is hell. In September of 2008, Joe Schwarz endorsed Mark Schauer the Democrat running against Walberg, the now incumbent in the general election. Suffice it to say, all hell broke loose on the Republican side with this maneuver and Joe was inundated with a barrage of emails, notes, cards, letters and calls by outraged Republicans indignant that he would endorse a Democrat. His response was classic Joe, being outspoken, blunt, humorous and priceless at the same time. Damn, I wish I had kept a copy of his retort which in essence was, "Once any of you have the f----ing balls to put your name on a ballot let me know." Let's say the country club Republican crowd had no response.

Fast forward to September 2017.

Everybody deserves a fair shot.

Congressman Dingell must have thought I would make a good candidate. My wife and kids were okay with it. I had a professional team ready to go. No personal financial issues in the way. It was really now a question of whether I was willing to stand up to the clarion challenge of Joe Schwarz. Did I have the f---ing balls to put my name on the ballot?

*"All politicians should have three hats –
one to throw into the ring, one to talk through
and one to pull rabbits out of if elected."*
**Carl Sandburg**

# Chapter 6

Running for Congress has become a full-time and year round undertaking. If you are an elected official, re-election begins the day after you are elected, and for everybody else you give up your life from the get go. It shouldn't be that way, but it is the reality of campaigning today.

I decided to spend most of 2017 honestly exploring the notion of running. I say "honestly" since we often hear or see candidates "exploring" when we know full well they are running. My self-imposed fall deadline would allow me to move about at a variety of candidate events and forums and meet with political and community leaders to get a feel for how my message and overall candidacy would be received. It would also allow me to get a first-hand view of my potential primary opponents, evaluate their strengths and weaknesses and gauge how I might stack up in the primary on August 7, 2018. Finally, by waiting until fall, we might have a better idea of whether Congressman Fred Upton planned to run again, which was a critical factor in whether the race would be winnable. I was genuinely exploring. I had no interest in sending a message or any other such poppycock. Run and win or don't run.

Picnics, forums, lunches, coffees, house parties were the routine in 2017. Whether it was a "should I do this," lunch with former Kalamazoo County Administrator Peter Battani or the untold number of "let me introduce myself" coffees, it often felt like I was eating and caffeinating my way to Congress. They seem to never end. Each of the six counties would have some sort of Democratic Party gathering which would be part social, but with an opportunity for candidates to introduce themselves. Candidates would include those of us running or considering running for Congress, state House and Senate candidates, as well as possible gubernatorial contestants and others seeking state-wide office, in addition to numerous county and local officials. Often it seemed like the candidates outnumbered everybody else. I put a lot of miles on my car, but in doing so came to realize how much I enjoyed actually campaigning (not fundraising – more on that later) and the opportunity to meet, talk, listen and learn from others.

The Democratic field for the 6th Congressional District took shape in early 2017, and it looked like it would be six of us battling it out for the nomination if I joined the scrum (a seventh candidate, Aida Gray, would join the race in 2018, but quickly withdraw). My five competitors were:

*David Benac* – a positive firebrand. The 44-year-old Ph.D. history professor at Western Michigan University was a Bernie Sanders acolyte. A true believer in the Sanders' cause and a rebel Democrat who admitted voting for Jill Stein of the Green Party in the last presidential election. He disdained fundraising while pronouncing it was time "to return politics to the people." His strategy for victory was "doors, doors, doors" while mobilizing the Bernie Sanders army. It was to be grassroots, guerilla warfare insurrection directed at the establishment. He would challenge the status quo, whether it was the state or national Democratic Party or the Republicans.

*Paul Clements* – another Ph.D. professor from Western Michigan University who thought the third time would be the charm. He had run twice before against Upton in 2014 and 2016 losing by considerable margins both times (55% - 40% and 58% - 36%), but argued his experience would pay off this time. He, like Benac, came from the far left Sanders wing of the party. What he touted as his strength – experience – was also a major criticism in that he had run twice before and not even come close. An intelligent, dedicated man with significant name recognition that would make him a formidable opponent.

**Rich Eicholz** – was always somewhat of a political enigma to me. Both personable and well-educated with a Ph.D. in biology, Rich always reminded me of your favorite uncle. He was the oldest candidate at 69 (I was second oldest at 66) and the CEO of Cumulus LLC, which was a technology company involved in electric vehicle charging. His residence was what I think was a former summer home in New Buffalo which was far from the epicenter of the 6th Congressional District Democratic politics in Kalamazoo. As best as I could discern, he had never really been involved in politics. His platform was based on growing the renewable energy industry, which in turn would create thousands of jobs. He positioned himself as a businessman that would attract moderate Republicans, which he believed, as did I, would be critical for success in November of 2018. I was always perplexed as to how he envisioned a path to victory. He did not raise much money nor did he have the following of a Benac or Clements. Neither fish nor fowl. I would find out after the primary he tried to raise money, but without much success.

**Eponine Garrod** – aka Eppy – was 23-years-old when she announced she was running for congress. (She would turn 25 before the November 2018 election, making her constitutionally eligible for a seat in Congress). A self-proclaimed representative of the millennial generation and self-appointed, most progressive in the race, she had moved to the Kalamazoo area after securing a degree in chemistry from Michigan Tech University and worked as a quality control tester at Pfizer. Declaring her youth and gender would be an advantage, she was quick to espouse the laundry list of progressive causes/issues currently in fashion. She reminded me of the character Lucy in the comic strip Peanuts. No, not for some political version of Lucy pulling the football away from Charlie Brown, but more from the personality traits of Lucy who would quickly and assuredly pontificate sententiously on any question, concern or issue from what she called her "real in" psychiatric booth. Eppy was a dogged campaigner for the 14 or so months she was a candidate until, ironically, for someone who claimed to be a candidate of the people, she did not secure enough signatures to qualify for the ballot.

*Matt Longjohn* – is a 46-year-old resident of Portage who sought to use his medical degree and health background as the pillars of his campaign. "As a physician and health leader, I felt it was my duty to get into this race," he extolled in the *Detroit News* when making his announcement. (The use of the word "physician" and his status as a medical doctor would become a major issue in the general election). A graduate of Tulane Medical School and former National Health Officer of the YMCA, he anticipated correctly that his medical background would be a strong card to play in both the primary and general elections with a focus on The Affordable Care Act and pre-existing conditions. He spun quite the Horatio Alger life story. His father was a janitor, mother was a gym teacher and his family had walked to Southwest Michigan in the frontier days. He told audiences that his first wife was a drug addict and that he went through medical school as a single dad relying on WIC and loans to get through. He eventually married his high school sweetheart and they moved to the family farmhouse in Vicksburg before moving to Portage in 2010. He presented himself as the new generation of leadership. Something about him reminded me of former Senator John Edwards (D-NC).

This was the field in September of 2017, and my time to fish or cut bait was fast approaching. I had been exploring for quite a few months and had been careful not to trigger anything under the law that would make me a "candidate" which would in turn require filings and reports. I heard rumblings that there was talk that I should have formally declared, so I decided to call an old political friend, Mark Brewer, for advice. Mark was the former head of the Michigan Democratic Party and in my estimation the top election lawyer in the state. I explained to him what I had been doing and he assured me that I was safely ensconced in the "exploring" category and had no legal or ethical issues to worry about. When I asked him what I owed him for his services, he responded (if not verbatim, very close),

"George, after all you have done for Democrats and the party over the years, nothing. If you decide to run, you can hire me then." Forget the money. That reaction and those comments meant a lot to me. I clearly had a reservoir of goodwill in Democratic circles, but it begged the question. Was I going to throw my hat into the ring?

*"My choice early in life was between whether to be a piano player in a whorehouse or a politician, and to tell the truth, there's hardly any difference."*

**Harry S. Truman**

# Chapter 7

Running for Congress is tantamount to starting a small business quickly and hoping it doesn't remain that way for long. Obviously, financing a campaign is quite different than your normal small business, but aside from that, many of the basics are the same. First, you need a product of service to sell, which in a campaign is the candidate (bringing to mind the 1968 book, *The Selling of the President* by Joe McGinnis). You will then need an office, i.e., headquarters and whether it is your kitchen table or a full blown office with all the accoutrements that entails. Computers, phones, desks, chairs, printer and website are all part of the necessary mix. In addition, you will need a checking account, credit/debit cards, health benefits and record keeping in preparation for filings with state and federal tax authorities not to mention contribution reports due to the Federal Election Commission. Once this enterprise is up and running, having started both a small business and campaign, I assure you that one day you will wake up and say to yourself, "My God, what have I done?"

It all starts with people. I started with Annie Brown. Maybe, more accurately, Annie Brown started with me. You gotta love Annie. I did and do. She is an intrepid political junkie or as she would say, "Her drug of choice was politics." She remembered me from years before when she was a staff assistant for Senator Carl Levin (D-MI) and I was a young lawyer/lobbyist who would stop by his office. Unbeknownst to me they found my slight Southern twang quite amusing, but aside from the entertainment factor, according to Annie, they knew Senator Levin liked me so they were always quite welcoming. Fast forward to 2014, married with three children Annie ran unsuccessfully for state representative in the South Haven area where she lived. During her campaign, I would often drive through the neighboring town of Bangor and see the red and white campaign signs which boldly, but simply said, "Annie." I never put it together that it was her until I ran into her at the grocery store when she was running again in 2016. Once again the red and white Annie signs punctuated the rural landscape. I immediately fired off a contribution only to find out, to my chagrin, there was another Annie Brown running and I had sent it to the wrong one. No idea who she is, but hope she appreciated the contribution. Once I realized the mistake, I sent another contribution to the "right" Annie Brown. Regretfully, Annie lost the second time around in what is a tough district for Democrats.

On May 10, 2017, I met with Annie at the Biggby Coffee shop in South Haven to talk with her about my interest in running. Her spirit was infectious. Never one to be deterred, her feistiness roused in me an attitude of I could do this. Her enthusiasm combined with the more analytical approach of say Mark Schauer or B.J. Neidhardt encouraged me to forge ahead. The meeting was fun and invigorating, and I wrapped it up by commenting how much I enjoyed her campaign signs with the bold and simple "Annie."

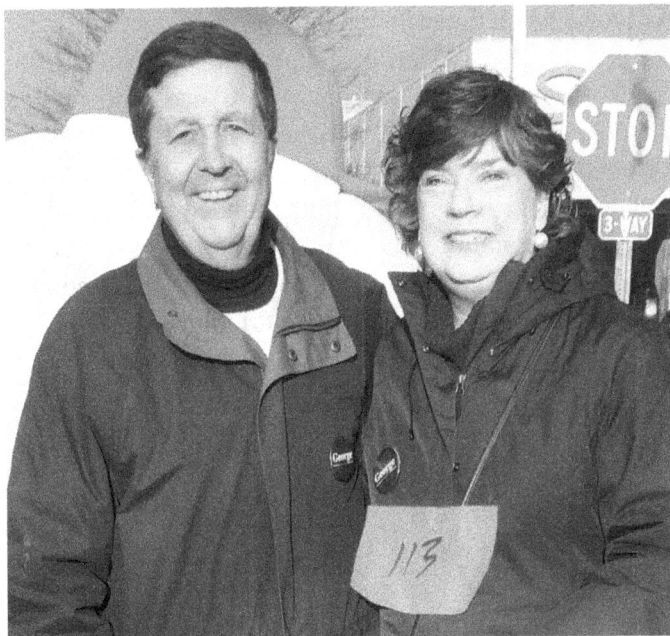

*Here I am with the indefatigable Annie Brown.*

Exactly a month later, on my birthday June 10, I celebrated by hosting a bipartisan Great Lakes policy conference at our home with the League of Conservation Voters (LCV). What better way to celebrate your birthday than to have two former congressmen – one a Republican and the other a Democrat – discuss water policy. Actually, it was an honor to host it with the League, which arguably is the most important and influential environmental organization in Michigan. This group is led by Lisa Wozniak, a dynamic president who served as co-host and moderator. It was a picture perfect day on Lake Michigan coupled with a lively attentive crowd and a robust discussion of Great Lakes issues. It was also a gathering that made me realize that the environment might be a political bridge to independents and moderate Republicans. All in all, it was a good day. As it concluded and we were telling our guests goodbye and see you later, Annie Brown strode up and handed me a campaign button which was simply the word "George" in bold letters.

*Campaign Pin*

A not so subtle message. That got my attention. Annie had the nerve to put her name on the ballot, and I thought to myself, okay how about you whiz bang.

Parades are an integral part of campaigns. Somewhat hokey, it is just part of what you need to do. Whether it is Memorial Day, 4th of July or Christmas, towns of all sizes have some sort of parade, and candidates are expected to be seen and for a candidate they really do give you a glimpse at a cross section of the district. My practice run on the parade circuit was helping carry the banner with Senator Debbie Stabenow at the Paw Paw Wine Festival Parade in September of 2017. That woman can sure work a parade. Nonstop energy on both sides of the street and the ability to blow past hecklers like they didn't exist. It was fun to watch, and it was fun to be part of her entourage with Paulette Porter an old friend from D.C. and a former Hill staffer who had moved back to Michigan. Watching Debbie and the assembled group in action left little doubt as to why she was such a successful politician and why she would win again in 2018. She was/is a tireless and excellent retail campaigner.

In mid-summer of my exploratory phase, I reconnected with Carol Heflin, a warhorse of liberal Democratic politics in Kalamazoo. Former chair of the Kalamazoo County Democratic Party, she was a close friend with former state Representative Ed LaForge (Ed died in January of 2018). Carol had great "cred" with the older establishment/labor wing of the party, and she knew me from years past when I was the corporate business person supporting such Democratic stalwarts as Ed LaForge, former Congressman Howard Wolpe, Governor's Blanchard, Granholm and others. She enthusiastically encouraged my candidacy and was more than willing to stand up when my Democratic bona fides were challenged. She was from the old school. Remember your friends. It also happened that her daughter-in-law, Shannon Sykes Nehring, was a member of the Kalamazoo City Commission and an outspoken leader of the African American community and progressive causes. (Shannon ended up endorsing David Benac which made sense given her politics, but she was always cordial and willing to advise. For whatever it was worth, she may have helped me establish a "well he is not that bad" reputation with some of the far left.) Carol and I agreed she would have a role in the campaign, which would need to be worked around her catering business, especially her responsibilities for meals at the Hope Woods Senior Living Center.

By September of 2017, I had met with an untold number of people and had been to more coffee shops in the 6th Congressional District then I ever imagined existed. Still no word on whether Fred Upton was in or out, but he was sounding and acting like someone who was getting ready to run for the U.S. Senate. I on the other hand was sounding and acting like someone who was going to run for the U.S. Congress.

*"A politician needs the ability to foretell what is going to happen tomorrow, next week, next month and next year. And to have the ability afterwards to explain why it didn't happen."*
**Winston Churchill**

## Chapter 8

"He is either going to run for the Senate or retire," according to Amey Upton, Fred's wife, as conveyed by a mutual friend from the Republican Leadership Conference in September 2017.

"Upton readies Senate bid," headlined Politico on September 15, 2017.

"On the island, Upton (R) St. Joseph, again raised the possibility that he'd join the race for the Senate seat, putting up sponsored ads with 'Upton 2018' slogans," reported MLive.

The "island" is 3.8 square mile Mackinac Island, the idyllic vacation spot located in Lake Huron between Michigan's lower and upper peninsulas. The island is famous for not allowing any motorized vehicles of any type (the UPS "truck" is a horse drawn carriage), a plethora of fudge shops (tourists are called fudgies) and is home to the Grand Hotel which boasts to have a 660 ft. front porch, the largest in the world. Politically, the island is significant as the location of the governor's summer residence where, in the summer of 1960, JFK famously secured the endorsement for president from Michigan Governor G. Mennen "Soapy" Williams. The island is also the site of the annual policy conference of the Detroit Regional Chamber as well as the Biannual Republican Leadership Conference, which is a cattle call for every Republican in the state considering running for anything, and September of 2017 was no exception. Fred Upton was seriously considering a run against incumbent U.S. Senator Debbie Stabenow. He first, however, would face a primary which appeared to include former Supreme Court Justice Bob Young, West Point/Army veteran John James and businessman Sandy Pensler. Whatever was the mix of candidates it would be expensive and, under the surface, a duel between the Trump forces and mainstream wings of the party. It would be ugly.

Fred Upton was, and is, a good, decent and thoughtful person. (One of the silliest statements made during the Democratic primary was in a fundraising letter written by one of my opponents who referenced

Fred, "As the monster he truly is." Just plain wrong and stupid. Hyperbole, which calls credibility on other issues into question). I never wanted to run against him and hoped to hell that he would, as Amey reportedly said, "Either run for the Senate or retire." I was running against Donald Trump to wrest control of the Congress from Republican/Trump control by flipping 23 seats from Republican to Democrat. I guess if Fred Upton had announced he was going to vote for a Democrat for speaker of the House, I might have folded my tent and gone home. I meant it when I said it at practically every candidate forum, house party, coffee – or you name it – when I commented in referring to the other Democratic primary candidates, "This is not about us. What this is about is flipping 23 seats and control the U.S. House of Representatives. The Republicans control the executive branch, the judiciary and the Senate, which theoretically could flip, but with 26 Democratic seats up in the Senate vs. nine Republicans it was highly unlikely. The only place to provide a check on this administration and inject some balance is the House of Representatives. The most important thing any of us will do if elected will be done in the first 15 minutes when we vote for a Democratic speaker. That is the game changer."

You can't wait forever, and reading the tea leaves on what a politician might or might not do is an exercise in futility. Late September was crunch time and I needed to commit go or no go; realizing, however, the political landscape might change, but also realizing that if I decided to run I would be in all the way. Five Democratic primary opponents, an incumbent who may or may not run, but appearing likely to hang it up surrounded by a bevy of Republican congressional wannabes waiting in the wings, portended a long tumultuous road ahead. I narrowed it down to three questions that needed to be addressed before making a decision:

1. Can I win?

2. What were the issues and how do they fit with my core beliefs?

3. Am I and is my family willing to be subjected to the rigors and scrutiny of a campaign?

I thought I could win. The juxtaposition of the first and second questions might seem out of order and somewhat mercenary, but I learned the importance of winning the hard way at a very early age. If you don't win, then what you believe and what you want to do is all for naught. I worked in the McGovern presidential campaign where our cause was to end the Vietnam War, reorder the nation's priorities and enact a slew of progressive causes. We were truth, justice and the American way. We got clobbered. The result was Richard Nixon, Cambodia, Vietnam and Watergate. I also worked for Roberto Reveles, the first significant Mexican American candidate for Congress in Arizona. He was a product of the farm workers' movement and as such was endorsed by Cesar Chavez. He was/is a wonderful person who if elected to Congress would have been a powerful advocate for minorities and other under-represented constituencies. Under-financed and under-resourced we never had a chance. We got clobbered.

It is never worth selling your soul to win, but you need to be practical. Flipping the 6th Congressional District would require support from outside the district, national resources if you would. I am not only talking money, but endorsements, visits and the like that would draw attention to the race, energize the base, but also give moderate Republicans and independents a rationale to change their voting habits and give a Democrat a try.

Looking at the primary field, I didn't see anyone with a national political network who could generate significant outside attention and support (the eventual nominee never did unlike Elissa Slotkin and Haley Stevens who successfully flipped seats in Michigan by, in part, accessing their national connections). However, to win the general election, you first have to win the primary, and I erroneously began my evaluation of potential success by comparing my history of community involvement with those of my primary opponents. It was a flawed premise upon which to evaluate potential success. I found out too late that people care less about what you have done and would rather listen to what you claim you will do regardless whether it is realistically attainable or not.

I had a national network that I could access if I got through the primary. My community involvement as a university trustee, supporter of Planned Parenthood, environmental advocate, member of economic development boards and notable involvement in criminal justice issues, I thought positioned me well in a primary.

The answer to the first question, can you win? It was doable.

As I mentioned before, I was not willing to sell my soul to win, so the question regarding the issues and whether my positions would be palatable in both the primary and general elections loomed large. None of this "pivot" nonsense after the primary. My positions on August 7 would be the same on November 6, but were they sellable? Post Jimmy Carter, the Democratic Party in districts like the 6th had suffered the onus of gays, guns and God – the three G's. My positions on the three G's were mainstream Democrat (my convictions on gay rights and gun issues were enhanced by experiences on the campaign which I will discuss later). Civil rights for the LGBTQ community, thoughtful and practical gun safety measures, a strong aversion to people who wear religion and morality on their sleeves, Dreamers, health care, Planned Parenthood, tariffs, campaign finance, Mexican walls and the environment all would be major topics of discussion. My position on these and other issues would place me in the center lane of Democratic politics, which means I would be left of center for the district. A problem in the general election, but one that was not insurmountable. My business background and resume would prove to be a detriment in the primary for those looking for a progressive archangel, but would be a plus in the general election.The rap on Democrats and their left leaning positions was that they were anti-business and not practical. I was a former corporate officer of Kellogg Company and had run my own small business for the past 12 years. What were they going to do call me anti-business? In fact, it used to irk me that so many Republicans who espoused all sorts of free market principles had never held a private sector job in their life. I actually looked forward to taking this hypocrisy in the most conservative areas of the district and calling their bluff.

My core beliefs put me safely within the acceptable zone for a Democratic primary and playing left field in the general election. My resume would make me suspect in the primary (the hell with my record), but on the other hand an asset in the general election. My months exploring a run had convinced me that Democratic primary voters sincerely wanted a candidate who could win and that a business person with a consistent Democratic ideology would pass muster.

If I ran, I was comfortable with my position on the issues and my ability to maintain my integrity while attracting the support I would need to win.

You and your family had better be able "to take a joke," we used to quip, if you run for Congress. You are going to get pummeled either fairly or unfairly. It is the sad reality of modern day campaigns. Nothing is off limits whether it has anything to do with your ability to do the job or should properly reside in the dustbin of history.

I was always glad Facebook and cell phones with cameras did not exist when I was going through college and law school, but aside from the normal indiscretions of youth, nothing disqualifying resided in my past. I had applied for and been granted a low-level security clearance in the Clinton administration, was a non-active member in good standing of the District of Columbia Bar and had twice been approved by the Michigan Senate as a constitutional officer of the state (Western Michigan University Board of Trustees). All in all, I had been vetted more than most people and came out clean. The difference between bar membership, security clearances and Senate confirmation and political attacks is that the former are based on facts as opposed to political attacks in which the facts be damned. Later in the campaign a shill for one of my opponents would go off half-cocked making claims without knowing or concerning themselves with the facts. Unfair yes, but damaging none the less in an era when accusations equal guilt and perceptions equal truth.

My wife Molly was totally supportive of my running knowing full well, from her past life in politics, what we were getting into. My daughters, both in their 30's, were old enough not to allow whatever they threw at me to materially affect them. Personally, I knew that my support in the past for Fred Upton and other Republicans would be an angle of attack as would my role as a corporate lobbyist. I used to laugh with friends on what the attack ads would look like. Gray grainy pictures of white males in suits going down the Capitol corridors with bags of money, while a deep-voiced narrator solemnly warns of backroom deals made by unscrupulous lobbyist. Total nonsense, but reality be damned.

One final aspect of diving into a fishbowl and a point worth a family discussion is the ramifications of the Stock Act of 2012. A legal requirement most candidates are unaware of and an obligation even over-looked by many incumbents. The lack of familiarity with this law is attested by the fact that in 2018, 116 candidates, including many members of Congress had not fulfilled their Stock Act requirement by the May 15 deadline.

The Stop Trading On Congressional Knowledge (Stock) Act of 2012 obligates anyone who raises or spends $5,000 running for Congress to provide de-tailed sources of income, assets and liabilities. Unlike Donald Trump, you have to provide voters with a full financial disclosure breakdown. The website of the Clerk of the House goes on to aver:

*"Section 8 of the Stock Act of 2012, as amended, requires the Clerk of the House of Representatives to provide online public access to Financial Disclosure*

*Reports filed by members of Congress
and candidates for Congress."*

In other words, you and your family's finances are now available for public scrutiny and dissection.

The Stock Act is invasive, but fair. My guess is that incumbents actually saw it as a positive in that it would give challengers one more thing to think about. Regardless of the politics, voters have a right to know of any real or perceived conflicts or self-dealings of those who hold elected office. I was quite comfortable with my financial success and making it public. It wasn't like I had inherited it, quite the contrary, I had earned it all on my own working full time since my college years.

I knew I would get hit, but I was comfortable enough in my own skin to take it. My wife and kids were good to go. Winning was doable and my beliefs were sellable. I was running for Congress.

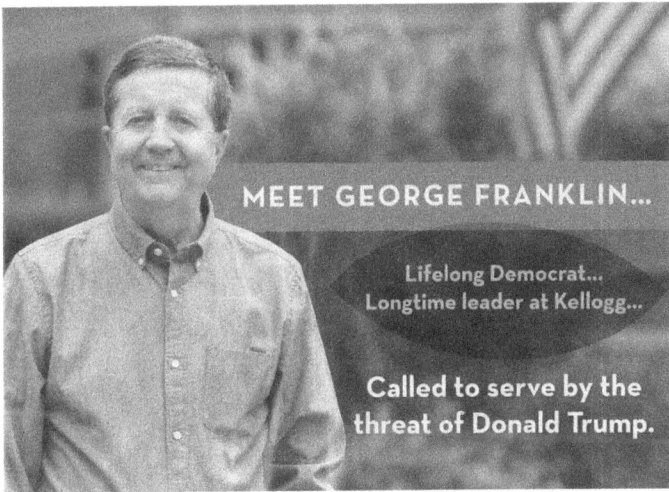

*Direct Marketing Piece*

*"He knows nothing and thinks he knows everything. That points clearly to a political career."*
**George Bernard Shaw (in Major Barbara)**

# Chapter 9

You've probably never heard of the *Paw Paw Courier* or the *Saugatuck Commercial Record*, but both newspapers were part of our announcement roll out. Sure, they are not *The New York Times* or *The Wall Street Journal*, but they are great community newspapers that provide meaningful local news that has a real impact on neighborhoods and people's day-to-day lives.

On October 4, 2017, we announced I was running for Congress in the Democratic Party in the 6th Congressional District of Michigan, and Annie and I hit the road. Following up on an old fashion press release accompanied by social media, we did drop-ins on numerous community papers – some dailies, but mostly weeklies. The announcement included more than 100 endorsements, including former Congressman Mark Schauer and was highlighted by a statement by former Governor Jim Blanchard: "George excelled as an appointee to the Board of Trustees at Western Michigan University. During his tenure the university expanded educational opportunities for Michiganders of all ages. No other candidate in the race has George's proven experience or track record in fighting for students and improving schools."

Quite a few of the community papers carried our announcement, usually accompanied by a picture which they took on the spot when we dropped in.

## Franklin plans run for District 6 U.S. House seat

George Franklin of Glenn has announced he will run as a Democrat for the U.S. District 6 House seat.

Franklin, 65, a businessman and attorney, is eying the seat held since 1993 by U.S. Rep. Fred Upton (R-St. Joseph). Upton is considering seeking the GOP U.S. Senate nomination in 2018 to run against incumbent Democrat Debbie Stabenow.

George Franklin

*Community Newspaper Coverage*

We also received good press coverage from the *Kalamazoo Gazette*, which is the largest daily in the district, as well as WWMT Channel 3 (the CBS affiliate) which is the most important TV station in the district. The Channel 3 coverage was about two minutes in length, which sounds short, but on the nightly news is actually quite long. The piece started with the anchor declaring that Fred Upton has a "new challenger" who, as a former vice president of Kellogg Company and a member of the Western Michigan University Board of Trustees and other volunteer efforts, has "a lot of ties to West Michigan." The video aspect of the coverage included a short scene of Annie and me walking down the sidewalk, stock photos of Kellogg headquarters and Western Michigan University and an interview with me where I mentioned my background in working with Democrats and Republicans, recruiting business and creating and maintaining jobs. The piece ended with a screen shot of my specific goals and areas of interest:

- Job Creation
- Ensuring Safe Workplaces
- Strong Schools
- Clear Drinking Water
- Affordable Health Care.

Pro-worker, pro-business, pro-environment, pro-schools and pro-health. Just about every pro you could want. Not a bad beginning, but now the hard part starts – building a plane while flying it.

Staffing a campaign is somewhat of an ad hoc process where the pieces are hobbled together through a combination of your friends and connections, referrals, references and volunteers. It grows organically around three pillars: a campaign manager, a finance director and a compliance manager.

As someone who came out of the business world, I was always struck that the function of a campaign manager would not easily fit into the typical management matrix. He or she works for you, but is also someone from whom you take orders and direction. For the rest of the staff it becomes a daily of whom is in charge question. Don't get me wrong, as the candidate you are ultimately responsible, but the day-to-day dynamics are a mixed blend of management decision making. The campaign manager better be someone you can trust and also someone whose company you enjoy because you are going to be spending a lot of time together.

I was fortunate to find a guy named Eli Isaguirre to be my campaign manager. Thirty-one years old, street smart, honest, personable and with enough experience to command the respect of others as the Franklin for Congress team came together. I had known him casually when he was the political "body man" for Mark Schauer when he ran for governor, a function similar to mine as a staffer for Congressman Frank Thompson (D-NJ) when I was in college and law school. It is a position of great trust and one in which you learn a lot. You are with the candidate every day and you see and hear almost everything. Eli had run unsuccessfully for state representative in the Flint area and was now the political director for the Michigan Nurses Association. He came with strong recommendations from Mark Schauer, B.J. and Annie, who had worked with him in her campaign. It was an easy decision which I never once regretted.

Yes, I will beat the dead horse again. It takes money to run a successful campaign and a lot of it.

Bernie Sanders supporters were justifiably critical of too much money in politics, but ironically, it cost him about $234 million to get that message out in his presidential campaign. Proving the caution by Will Rogers to would be candidates, "Politics has got so expensive that it takes lots of money to even get beat with." So true.

Your finance director has to figure out how to raise a lot of money and implement the plan to do so. He or she, in my case she, is selling you to a group of investors, some of whose intentions may be as pure as the driven snow, but some more mercenary. This is where Kathryn Tapper Scott comes into the picture (someone I affectionately nicknamed "coach" as a result of her rah-rah motivational speeches). I met Kathryn over Annie's breakfast table in South Haven and was immediately impressed by her energy and enthusiasm. She had worked for Annie in her state representative campaign and was looking to hitch her wagon to one of the congressional campaigns. She and her wife Kristy were expecting a baby, but she was confident she would have the time and energy to devote to a big time fundraising effort. She was creative, exuberant and committed. I was good to go with Kathryn as finance director.

The third pillar of any campaign is a compliance manager and, have no doubt, there is a lot to comply with, complicated by a plethora of designations and definitions. Individual, candidate committee, political action committees (PACs) both multicandidate and non-multicandidate, are just a few examples of potential donors who come with varying limitations and restrictions. The compliance manager has to be abreast of all this along with filing deadlines, House Ethics, as well as financial disclosure requirements all in the midst of a campaign which by definition is chaotic.

Heather Ricketts has created a business as a compliance manager for campaigns with an enviable cadre of clients. She had a track record of success when we brought her on to keep us on the straight and narrow. A large part of her job is being the enforcer, especially in regard to the candidate, campaign manager and finance director. She has to be able to tell people "no" a lot while making sure contributions, expenses and expenditures comply with federal and state law. It seems like the issues and questions are endless. For example, are cash contributions allowed? (Yes, but no more than $100 per person). May non-U.S. citizens contribute to campaigns? (No, unless they are green card holders). Federal government contractors may not contribute to federal elections. Husband and wife couples have separate contribution limitations even if only one spouse has an income. Do the costs associated with a house party constitute a contribution? (An individual may spend $1,000 per candidate – $2,000 per couple – per election for food and beverage, invitations, etc. for a house party without it constituting a contribution). It goes on and on.

How it all became so complicated is a Washington evolutionary tale of legislation and litigation fought out by special interests on the right and the left. Whether you approve or disapprove of the current campaign finance system, there is no dispute it is awash in funds and entails a herculean effort to keep track of. According to OpenSecrets.org, the 2,905 House of Representative candidates in the 2017-18 election cycle collectively raised to the tune of 1.5 billion dollars. The 1,511 Democrats raked in $180 million or so from PACs and $700 million plus from individuals, while the 1,220 Republican candidates enjoyed the largess of PACs in the neighborhood of $220 million and $350 million from individuals. Any way you cut it, a lot of money is flying around during elections.

The entity responsible for overseeing campaign contributions and reporting is a toothless tiger known as the Federal Election Commission comprised of six commissioners, serving six-year terms, appointed by the president and confirmed by the Senate. Its existence and the laws it enforces date back to the early 1970's and, in particular, the Watergate reforms encapsulated in the Federal Election Campaign Act of 1974. An act which placed limitations on campaign contributions and expenditures, but which were significantly modified and curtailed by subsequent Supreme Court decisions. Three decisions in particular stand out. The first was Buckley vs. Valeo in 1976, brought by former U.S. Senator James Buckley from New York who was a member of the Conservative Party. (He also was the brother of William F. Buckley, the conservative columnist and founder of the *National Review*.) In this case, the Supreme Court struck down limitations on candidate expenditures as violative of First Amendment Rights. This was followed by another attempt to limit campaign expenditures with the passage of the Bipartisan Campaign Reform Act of 2002, better known as McCain-Feingold after Senators John McCain (R-AZ) and Russ Feingold (D-WI). The legislation was an effort to limit issue advocacy containing the name of candidates 30 days before a primary and 60 days before a general election. Such communication was termed "electioneering communication" and banned under the act. When McCain-Feingold was challenged in McConnell vs. FEC in 2003, it was essentially upheld, albeit in a rather confusing, disjointed decision by the Supreme Court only to be in gist overturned in Citizens United vs. FEC in 2010 with a 5-4 decision. On First Amendment grounds, Citizens United authorized independent expenditures by corporations, labor unions and other legal entities so long as they were not done in coordination with campaigns. In other words, they allowed the creation of what we now call super PACs and an infusion of a lot more money into politics. If it all seems very confusing, join the club.

Per the FEC website, the following is a simplified version of where we stand in 2019:

### *Contribution Limits*
An individual may give a maximum of:

**$2,700 per election to a federal candidate** or the candidate's campaign committee.[2] Notice that the limit applies separately to each election. Primaries, runoffs and general elections are considered separate elections.

**$5,000 per calendar year to a PAC.** This limit applies to a PAC (political action committee) that supports federal candidates. (PACs are neither party committees nor candidate committees. Some PACs are sponsored by corporations and unions — trade, industry and labor PACs. Other PACs, often ideological, do not have a corporate or labor sponsor and are therefore called non-connected PACs.) PACs use your contributions to make their own contributions to federal candidates and to fund other election-related activities.

**$10,000 per calendar year to a state or local party committee.** A state party committee shares its limits with local party committees in that state unless a local committee's independence can be demonstrated.

**$33,900 per calendar year to a national party committee.** This applies separately to a party's national committee, House campaign committee and Senate campaign committee.

**$100 in currency (cash) to any political committee.** (Anonymous cash contributions may not exceed $50.) Contributions exceeding $100 must be made by check, money order or other written instrument.

Heather was a tough enforcer which was exactly what we wanted. As each new person, staff or volunteer came on board, we shared with them the notion that none of this, whether we won or lost, was worth compromising personal principles or stretching legal boundaries. I shared with them an adage that I had learned while learning to fly airplanes that was apropos to political campaigns. If it involved a legal, ethical or moral issue – when in doubt don't. Whatever seems so important now probably won't five months or five years from now and definitely will not if you do something you will regret down the road.

People get caught up in campaigns and politics and somehow lose their ethical bearings, a change which is also quite common if they end up going to D.C. It reminds me of some sage advice I received as a young staffer from a Hill veteran named Bill Cable. Bill was dispatched by Speaker Tip O'Neill to the Carter White House to revamp the congressional relations function which was in disarray under a group of aides who were quite full of themselves. After Bill had been at the White House for a few months, I asked him what he had identified as the root of the problem and he replied, "They don't understand that this all ends sometime." They needed to treat people with respect and understand that the decisions they made and how they treated other people will last well beyond their years in the White House. Just ask a guy named John Dean, who worked for a president named Nixon and lost his bearings.

Eli the campaign manager was a pillar, but he was actually preceded as a staffer by the rock of the campaign, A.J. Ennis. One other staffer later referred to her as the campaign MVP. All of us, especially me, are forever indebted to A.J. Steadfast, diligent and dedicated, A.J. was a 22-year-old graduate of Women's Studies at Western Michigan University. She was another product of the Annie Brown for state representative campaign where she had worked with Kathryn as field director and assistant campaign manager. In our campaign, she was going to be call time manager

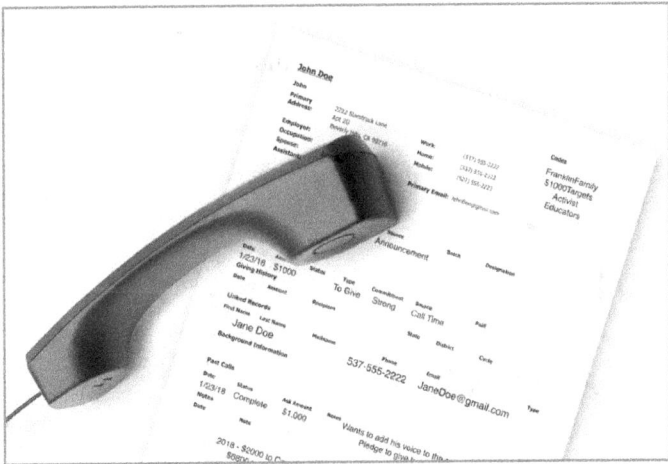

*Sample Call Time Sheet*

which is the political equivalent of running a torture chamber lacking only a rack and waterboarding device. Call time is the day-to-day grind of raising money and, as indicated by the name, you do it by making phone calls. Thousands of calls, 12,991 to be exact, which did not include sundry calls made outside of call time.

How A.J. persevered through all this with me, I will never know. She would start each day by flopping open a binder which contained a 100 or so call sheets she had prepared the day before. It made you wish you had a dental appointment. Each call sheet would have the name, number and past giving history of each individual as well as notes or tidbits ("she has a dog named Sue").

It would go on for hours and she would have to listen to me give the same spiel and tell the same stories ad nauseam. I finally asked her point blank one day, how could she do this and she succinctly replied, "I want to win."

*A.J. surviving another day of call time.*

A.J. and I had some great laughs, especially when we would get punchy late in the day after a 100 or so calls. She would post fun and quirky stuff we would encounter on the call time room walls. One of our favorites was a recording when we called a fellow named Ned and the recording was something out of a Schlocky horror movie. "Ned is somewhere, but you will never know where." Hello Stephen King. Another quip we would do with each other was, "Let's call Nina." Nina was a call we had made from some list and the recipient – Nina – was not happy. In fact, she went ballistic. The problem was that it wasn't Nina, but someone else and the poor woman was getting barraged by political calls thinking she was Nina the contributor. I also used the call time to get techie advice a 66-year-old guy needed from a smart 22-year-old. Once A.J. was done instructing me to do whatever, I would usually say something to the effect, "Well, you millennials really are good for something," which became a running joke after she would jump into the fray, fix the problem after which I would feign understanding what she was doing.

I was known in the campaign for arriving early to everything. It was ingrained in me at a young age that it was disrespectful to others to be late, in effect kind of sending a message that my time is more important that yours. It also stemmed from being the youngest of four children who was afraid I might miss something or be left out. However, the only thing I was late for, now and then, was call time and if it wasn't for a delightful, dedicated person named A.J., I would have been late more often.

The Franklin for Congress core team would include three others from disparate backgrounds.

Zac Andrews was another Schauer campaign connection that along with Kathryn and A.J. completed the finance team. A Battle Creek guy, Zac joined the campaign in March of 2018 having worked in a red to blue race (more on that later) in Nebraska and also the Russ Feingold Senate race in Wisconsin in 2016. His title with us was finance assistant, but with his ability to track down any name from the past, I predict he will be in charge of the White House switchboard with the next Democratic president. If I remembered someone from the past, whether it was law school, the Hill, a lobbying connection or even old girlfriends; he could track them down and they would be on one of the dreaded call sheets that A.J. would torture me with. Zac was steady, even tempered, engaging and a hold-the-fort-down kind of guy.

Matthew Craig will be a professor some day and a damn good one. He is a natural. He will also always be an activist and it is the combination of these two attributes that brought him to the campaign. His LinkedIn page identifies causes and issues he "cares about" to include civil rights and social action, economic empowerment, human rights, politics and the elimination of poverty. Prior to joining the campaign, Matthew had been a Western Michigan University volunteer for the Kalamazoo County Democratic Party and active with the Michigan Coalition for HIV Health and Safety. He was organized, thoughtful, methodical and whiteboard at the ready. Matthew was field director for Kalamazoo County, the most populous and Democratic in the 6th Congressional District.

Finally, there was John Martin, volunteer extraordinaire who eventually would become paid staff. His title was special events, which was appropriate since he was/is special. Every organization needs a personality that can provide a spark and a lift when the mood is morose. Always upbeat and ready to lighten the atmosphere with a quip, John was that person. He worked in the evenings as a waiter at Fandango, an upscale Kalamazoo restaurant and would come in the next morning with stories about who from the political world had been there and what they said. He would usually end the story by telling the customer, "I work for George Franklin for Congress." John was an invaluable asset to the campaign.

Eli, Annie, Kathryn, Heather, A.J., Carol, Zac, Matthew, and John, would comprise the core team with 3 field operatives and volunteers coming on board later as the campaign progressed. We were off and running.

*Left to right: John, Annika, Charlie, A.J., Matthew, Kathryn and Eli making fun of my old age on my birthday.*

*"Politics is not the art of the possible.
It's the art of choosing between
the disastrous and the unpalatable."*
**John Kenneth Galbraith**

# *Chapter* 10

Once you announce your candidacy, hang on for what is sure to be the rollercoaster ride of your life, minus the seat belt. Coffees, forums, meet and greets and the proverbial chicken dinners will be the norm and all this while you have to financially feed the monster called a campaign. What could be more fun than call time for four hours on New Year's Eve?

My schedule from early October 2017 until the end of December included 125 hours of call time and not quite 100 "events." A term I use loosely since an "event" included everything from coffee with one city commissioner to the 'Best of the West' Michigan Democratic Party dinner in Grand Rapids with 600 attendees. Generally, activities fit into the broad categories of parades, group functions (e.g. League of Women Voters), fundraisers, meet and greets, forums and one on one's in the ubiquitous coffee shop setting. It was a time of meeting a lot of interesting people, reviving old acquaintances and tracking down people you haven't seen or spoken to in years. It was also a period in which you honed your stump speech while refining your position on the issues. Everything the campaign was all about began to take shape.

When Senator Ted Kennedy first ran for president, he was infamously tripped up by a simple, straightforward question asked by noted TV journalist Roger Mudd, "Why do you want to be president?" Senator Kennedy stammered, hemmed and hawed in his response, leaving viewers with the impression that he really didn't know why he wanted to be president, or worse yet, he wanted to be president because he wanted to be president. He had no purpose. Likewise, when you run for Congress, people expect and deserve an answer to the simple question, "Why do you want to be a member of Congress or, in more simple terms, "Why the hell are you doing this?"

My reason reached back to that fellow I mentioned before who years ago walked into the Special Subcommittee on Labor looking for a job. He wasn't looking for special treatment or privilege; all he was looking for was a "fair shot." His story and the notion of a "fair shot" became the prologue of my stump speech, my forum remarks and the signature slogan of my campaign. It encapsulated why I was running. Senator Carl Levin had advised me months before to be authentic, and the authentic me was running on the simple premise that everyone deserved a fair shot in their pursuit of health, wealth and happiness.

At practically every event, I would begin by telling the story of that guy in the Subcommittee office looking for a job and how to give him a fair shot which then allowed me to address the litany of issues of what did or did not constitute a fair shot.

You don't have a fair shot if the tax code is skewed to help the rich at the expense of the poor and the middle class.

You don't have a fair shot if the education system isn't properly funded and teachers don't receive the compensation and respect they deserve.

You don't have a fair shot without proper access to health care, which is a fundamental human right just like food, clothing and shelter.

You don't have a fair shot without a safe working environment, a living wage and the right to bargain collectively.

I would invoke the same fair shot mantra as it applied to gun violence, Planned Parenthood and reproductive rights, tariffs and trade, civil rights, economic disparity/injustice and campaign finance depending on the audience interest or questions.

My epilogue would be to emphasize that this race wasn't about me or any of the other candidates, but rather was about flipping 23 seats in the House of Representatives from Republican to Democrat thereby changing control. That was the game changer. The Trump Republicans had control of the executive branch, the Senate theoretically could flip from Republican to Democrat, but with the mix of seats up in 2018 that was very unlikely and with the Supreme

Court and the judiciary being filled with sympathetic judges, the Republicans controlled all three branches of government. The only place to provide a check and some balance to the Republican agenda was in the House of Representatives and this could only occur by a Democratic majority. I reiterated that the reality was that the most important thing any of us could do would be done in the first minutes of the term when we voted for a Democratic speaker. To secure that opportunity, however, we first had to win, and it was going to take more than a blue wave to win in the 6th Congressional District of Michigan. We had to give independents and moderate Republicans somewhere to go. Similar to what Doug Jones had successfully done in getting elected to the U.S. Senate in Alabama and although I was no Doug Jones, my corporate and small business background gave me entree to constituents not before amenable to a Democrat. Simply put, I thought I could win.

(Rich Eicholz and I were the only two candidates focusing on the need to attract independents and Republicans as a path to victory. The other candidates were counting on the blue wave to be of sufficient force to deliver victory. What they didn't factor in was the magnitude of the red tide outside of Kalamazoo.)

We never had what I would call a debate since the number of candidates (six, and for a while, seven) precluded much one-on-one interaction, but we had quite a few forums/panels. These forums came under

the auspices of a variety of groups and generally followed the same format, whether we were in a church
basement or a school gym, we sat at a long table in
front of the audience with three mics and seating for
each candidate behind their name card. Each candidate
would be allowed a couple of minutes for an opening
statement after which the moderator would ask each
candidate the same question rotating who was asked
the question first. Although the questions would vary
somewhat depending on what was topical in the
news, the core issues – health care, environment, gun
violence, immigration and campaign finance reform
would be rather consistent and included in each
candidate's opening and closing remarks. After a half
dozen or so forums, we knew each other's spiels so
well, we could have given them for each other. Rich
Eicholz was clean energy jobs, David Benac was
power back to the people and away from corporations,
Paul Clements was climate change, Matt Longjohn
was health care and Eponine Garrod was the self-proclaimed most progressive candidate and spokesperson
for the millennials.

These forums also provided the opportunity to
attack me for being a corporate lobbyist. A reference
made dripping with disdain and something I got quite
used to, but never reconciled with. To borrow some
football jargon, if David Benac, Rich Eicholz or Paul
Clements went after me for being a corporate lobbyist
those would be fair, clean hits, but when Matt Longjohn
or Eponine Garrod did so, which they did routinely,

they deserved a penalty flag for flagrant hypocrisy. I would sit there and take it, but had to bite my tongue in doing so.

Matt Longjohn, from the inception of his campaign, crowed about the work he did at the YMCA on national diabetes prevention programs. These programs were in part funded by the federal government, and I have been around Washington enough to know that these types of grants are not only based on the brilliance of the proposal, but usually involve some lobbying. Oh my God, yes lobbying. Well, sure enough, during the years Matt Longjohn was the national health director of the YMCA, they retained a group of lobbyists at an outfit called Cornerstone Government Affairs, which is a multi-client lobby shop in D.C. Cornerstone on their website boasts about securing federal funding for the diabetes programs Matt Longjohn was in charge of at the YMCA.

*"We have also worked to bring additional resources to the Diabetes Prevention Program – A partnership among the YMCA, private insurers, and the CDC – which brings the YMCA's adaption of the program at 1,700 sites, with over 50,000 participants in 47 states."*

If there is any doubt, in addition to the website, Cornerstone registered each year under the Lobby Disclosure Act with a six figure contract to lobby on behalf of the YMCA in regard to "Health and Wellness Issues in the Labor HHS Appropriations Bill." These same lobbyists, not surprisingly, contributed thousands of dollars to a rogues' gallery of right-wing Republicans focused on appropriations and Republican leaders of Congress (Fred Upton was a recipient one year) who were in the majority and controlled the purse strings.

Getting berated by Matt Longjohn for being a corporate lobbyist, considering the lobbying by the YMCA and his role there, was quite galling unless of course:

1. He was only the piano player or

2. Like Rick's Café in the movie Casablanca, he was unaware and shocked to know what was really going on.

My guess is that neither scenario is apropos and what we have is a clear, straightforward double standard.

Eponine Garrod, with all her didactic declarations on the high cost of drugs and health care, works for Pfizer, one of the largest drug companies in the world and one of the most aggressive lobby entities in the pharmaceutical industry. According to Open Secrets, in 2017 Pfizer spent $10,470,000 lobbying in D.C. and made political contributions to the tune of $2,374,462. In addition to the federal activity, the Corporate Reform Coalition reports, "In 2016, Pfizer has as many as 284 lobbyists registered to lobby in 48 states. According to a recent study that measured state lobbying by industry (normalized by calculating expenditures per $1 million of revenue) Pfizer came in as the second highest spender." Why do they do all this lobbying? Because it makes them money and that profit directly benefits Eponine Garrod in the form of what in the vernacular is referred to as a paycheck. Corporate profits are derived from a variety of functions contributing to the bottom line. One such function is lobbying which inures to the benefit of all employees at all levels. It is disingenuous, to say the least, to attack someone for being a corporate lobbyist while you are personally and financially benefiting from what corporate lobbyists do on your behalf.

Lobbying, which is a constitutional right, is not the issue, but rather what causes and issues you lobby on behalf of is the question. If you are against lobbying, you are against the activities of Planned Parenthood, the League of Conservation Voters and Everytown for Gun Safety. I was proud of the lobbying I did to secure funding for cancer research, increased food safety and to promote economic development in Southwest Michigan. I am also proud of the work I did representing Kellogg Company, which spawned and funded the W.K. Kellogg Foundation, which is one of the major philanthropic organizations in the world. When I was in charge of Government Relations for Kellogg Company, more than 30% of our stock was owned by the Kellogg Foundation, loosely translating into one-third of our profits going to charity.

Considering the extensive lobbying of the YMCA and Pfizer while being attacked, it was difficult to maintain my sangfroid, but I believe I did for the most part. A calculated response which in hindsight I now question. Two people with halos is not much different than the Moral Majority wearing religion on their sleeves.

October, November and December 2017 were a swirl. Meet and greets, fundraisers, parades, dinners, coffees, new people, old acquaintances were all part of the mix. How many people can claim participation in the Goose Festival Parade in Fennville, walking with Santa in Paw Paw, joining the St. Joseph Reindog Celebration and marching in the Bangor Christmas Parade? Not to mention the Veterans Day Dinner in South Haven (where I met James C. McCloughan who had recently been presented the Medal of Honor by President Trump), the Progressive Women's Alliance brunch in Grand Rapids, the Brown-Todd-Wolpe Democratic Party dinner in Kalamazoo, as well as the "Best of the West" Michigan Democratic Party Gala in Grand Rapids, the NAACP Annual Dinner in Kalamazoo and the Berrien County League of Women Voters holiday dinner. All sorts of interesting people that teach you the dance of life through their stories, interests, hardships and activities.

Don Cooney is an 80-year-old professor in the School of Social Work at Western Michigan University, a Kalamazoo City Commissioner, but more importantly a warhorse of activist Democratic politics and a wonderful human being. At first blush you wouldn't think he and I would have much in common. An activist professor and a corporate officer are not a natural pair, but looks can be deceiving, and we shared some history. When I was a member of the Western Michigan University Board of Trustees, the university administration was advocating some anti-union, anti-worker initiatives which became the subject of vociferous demonstrations by Don and his cohorts. Union leaders came to me and my fellow trustee, Lana Boldi of the United Auto Workers (UAW) looking for support and, as a result, we broke rank with the other trustees in opposing the administration and aligning ourselves with Don and his group. (Fast forward, Lana was quick to endorse my run for Congress. She liked to say, "Franklin, it was you and me against the world." Hyperbole, but it often was just the two of us.)

I met with Don in October of 2017 at the Water Street Coffee Joint in Kalamazoo which was fast becoming my home away from home. I knew there was an outside chance I could secure his endorsement, but regardless it would be an opportunity to learn his take on the issues and the positions of the activist community. We talked for a good hour or so and reminisced about people, the university, issues and activities over the years. He remembered me as "the guy who stood with us," which was heartening, but when the idea of endorsement came up, he went on to explain that he had already endorsed his academic colleague David Benac. We sat for a while and regaled each other with political stories (my favorite "Cooney Caper" was when he was working on a state representative race and was to pick up the candidate for a major meeting with the newspaper editorial board and he went MIA. His problem was that he got arrested for demonstrating against apartheid in South Africa and was, you might say, a little tied up when he was supposed to be picking up the candidate.)

Wrapping up the conversation, I mentioned that David Benac seemed like a good man and I understood his support for him, but I wondered whether he might be willing to tell some of his progressive activist friends that I wasn't all that bad. This request engendered a chuckle and the response that he would be glad to do so. Months later, Don came to a fundraiser I had at Arcadia Brewery and made a very modest contribution which meant a lot to me. It wasn't the money, but his presence that counted. While he continued to support David Benac, showing up at Arcadia Brewery may have been his way of signaling to some that I wasn't all that bad. Don Cooney was and is a first class guy.

Campaigning you meet people who work tirelessly to make a difference in their communities. One such couple is Dr. Eric Lester and his wife Audrey. (I believe they both ended up supporting Matt Longjohn). Leaders in the Berrien County Democratic Party, they are also active in a community organization called Advocates and Leaders for Police and Community Trust (ALPACT), which is comprised of representatives from law enforcement, non-profits, community organizations and generally all walks of life. Meeting on a regular basis, participants in ALPACT address vexing social justice issues affecting the Benton Harbor – St. Joseph area. I attended a few of the meetings and always left encouraged that aside from all the political noise there were people working day to day to create positive change in their communities. It was at an ALPACT meeting that I met Mary Jo Schnell, executive director of the OutCenter in Benton Harbor. Subsequent to the meeting, Annie and I made a point to visit the facility which is a safe haven for the LBGTQ community and an organization with a vision to make Southwest Michigan a place where they and their families are "welcome, respected, valued, understood and afforded the same rights and responsibilities as everyone else." It is wonderful that the OutCenter exists, but sad that it is needed. Audrey Lester, Eric Lester and Mary Jo Schnell are role models for civic engagement.

I wish I'd had more meet and greet/house party type events. I enjoyed the format which allowed me to give my pitch, answer questions and genuinely have conversations and discussions. Not to sound too hokey, but they really are what campaigns and elections should be all about. Retail politics. Like the one Elisa Dely hosted for me at her home in early October. Elisa is a dynamic woman who has her own fitness company and is someone I have known casually for years. She was interested in my campaign and offered to help, but like most people had never held a "political" event. My rejoinder was to invite friends, family, neighbors, whether favorably disposed or not, keep it casual, and if we got more than five people we would count it as a win. In fact, about a dozen or so were gathered in her living room that evening with an attractive layout of hors d'oeuvres she had made in the adjoining dining room. I did okay, not great, and the reaction, I am guessing, was a mixed bag. I remember thinking, on the drive home, that it is people like Elisa, who are willing to wade into the political pond, that maintain a wholesomeness in the political process.

Carol Heflin and Peter Battani organized a get together for me in late November of 2017 with the more progressive Democrats, or what we affectionately referred to as the "lefties." Carol, as I mentioned before, had cred with this group from a lifetime of involvement in what used to be called liberal, pro-union politics. Peter had a career of civic engagement which resulted in him serving as Kalamazoo County administrator for years. (Peter is quite the character as someone who is totally unfiltered. He became a great friend and sounding board during the campaign. One day he took umbrage when I referred to him as half crazy. His riposte was, "What do you mean only half?") The group assembled was about two dozen or so activists seated in sort of the round in a dining hall with me standing in the middle. Not exactly a friendly forum – think coliseum without the lions. Ironically, I enjoyed it. Tough questions from knowledgeable people made it an invigorating afternoon. Also, as a result of the "Carol and Peter forum," Kathryn Tapper Scott and I had coffee at

Water Street Coffee Joint (yes, Water Street again) with Jen Strebs who is the progressive activist, founder of a political organization known as Prokzoo and a member of the Kalamazoo Township Board of Trustees. I learned a lot having coffee with her. Although she and I operated on different bandwidths, I found her to be smart, sincere and dedicated to her causes, and her comments made me look at some issues from a different angle. Health care policy was where we confronted the widest chasm in our views (if I remember correctly, she was a proponent of single payer and I was a fix Obamacare guy), but we discerned we actually were in sync on a lot of topics. I am pretty certain she supported someone else, but I will always appreciate her willingness to talk and listen.

Honorable Bill Schma is one of the most esteemed members of the legal community in Kalamazoo and his wife Gerry is a highly respected former administrator at Western Michigan University. I had known Gerry in my role as a trustee at the university and had worked with Bill when he became a judge trying to establish the drug courts which was a movement in which he would become a national leader. My participation in helping to create the drug courts was something I am still very proud of and an aspect of my background that I would reference in every presentation by relating a story of when Judge Schma and his Republican Counterpart Judge Hoffman came to enlist my help. In tandem they explained the situation.

Judge Hoffman described their reality as one where they sit on a bench with black robes dispensing justice, when they actually should be wearing white coats with tongue depressors in their pockets. Eighty percent of the people who come before them have some sort of drug or alcohol addiction problem. What they did next, according to both judges, was nonsensical. They would sentence the "criminal" to two or three years in prison at a cost to the taxpayers of $36,000 per year and when they were released the recidivism rate was 80% and they would go back doing exactly what they were doing before. A circular process that does nothing for the individual or society. On the other hand, if they were in a drug court which required treatment rather than jail, the cost to the taxpayer would be approximately $12,000 per year and the recidivism rate a low 20%. This would save lives and save money at the same time.

Bill and Gerry hosted a well-attended coffee for me at their home in the fall of 2017 during a period when I was getting my sea legs. In attendance was D. Terry Williams, the former chair of the Department of Theatre at Western Michigan University and without question the most highly regarded authority on acting and theatre in Southwest Michigan. Evidently I must not have been too sharp since after my pitch someone suggested that I get with D. Terry for some advice/coaching on delivery. D. Terry magnanimously agreed to help, and although we never did get together, it brought to mind an admonition I learned from Drew Marquardt, an up and coming Hollywood writer, "You have to hide spinach in the popcorn." Substance is important, but so is delivery and the message has to be more than doom and gloom. I had worked in the Carter presidential campaign in Atlanta in 1976 and was a fan of his. One major difference, however, between Carter and Reagan as they campaigned in 1980 was that Ronald Reagan, the former actor, understood that politics was part theater. Carter was the "country is suffering a national malaise" candidate and Ronald Reagan was "the USA is a shining city on a hill" candidate. One inspiring the other demoralizing. Never took a class from D. Terry Williams, but I learned a lesson that day.

Nothing in the fall of 2017 was more impactful than the endorsement of Senator Carl Levin and his appearance at a fundraiser for me in Kalamazoo on November 27. He is one of the two most-respected political figures in Michigan. The other being a Republican former Governor Bill Milliken. Carl Levin and the word integrity are interchangeable. Two unrelated stories immediately come to mind.

When I was a young lawyer/lobbyist in D.C. with Kellogg Company there was a major tax overhaul bill under consideration that was worth millions of dollars to the bottom line. The financial ramifications were such that our very Republican Chairman and CEO Bill LaMothe asked me to arrange a meeting with Senator Levin so that he could explain the importance of the legislation to Kellogg. Bill LaMothe, Senator Levin, an aide and I met for almost an hour at the Senator's office in the Russell Senate Office Building. Senator

Levin explained in great detail why he opposed the legislation and could not support the company's position. Not the outcome we had hoped for, but our chairman's reaction flying back to Battle Creek is what I will always remember. As Chairman and CEO, Bill LaMothe was not told "no" very often and even though Senator Levin had just done so, Bill commented to me, "I like that guy." We met with the Senator two other times on the tax bill with the same result and each time on the way back, I got the same rendition of, "I like that guy." Thoughtful and deliberate. He said no with integrity.

In 2007, I was in Atlanta with my wife Molly for the unveiling of a statue in honor of her former boss Republican U.S. Senator Paul Coverdell. Among the assorted dignitaries present was Republican U.S. Senator Johnny Isakson. I introduced myself as Molly's husband and explained I was from Michigan. Considering the setting (and my wife's politics), it would be quite normal for Senator Isakson to assume I was a Republican. Not knowing I was a Democrat, when hearing I was from Michigan, he immediately volunteered what a class act Carl Levin was and what a gentleman he was to work with. As I said Carl Levin and the word integrity are interchangeable.

His endorsement would be a huge boost for any campaign and especially for one in which the candidate was subject to the "is he really a Democrat" attack.

The Levin endorsement also created an opportunity for me to go seek the support of George Todd and his wife Clare, as well as Caroline Ham, who had been married to George's deceased father Paul and was the first female mayor of Kalamazoo. George is chairman of Kalsec which is a gem of a company headquartered in Kalamazoo that produces "natural spice and herb flavor extracts, colors, antioxidants and advanced hop products for the food and beverage industry." The Todd family connection with Carl Levin stemmed from Paul Todd having been a one-term member of Congress (1964 Johnson landslide), long time party leader and dear friend of the senator.

Not only did George and Clare agree to support me, but they were also willing to host my Levin fundraiser in their conference hall. If someone had told me back in those young lawyer, lobbyist days that Senator Carl Levin would be coming to Kalamazoo to host a fundraiser for me, I would have told you that you were out of your mind. However, sure enough, arriving on Amtrak from Detroit the afternoon of November 27 was Carl Levin, the former chairman of the Senate Armed Services Committee with his hair flopping to the side, his trademark glasses perched on the end of his nose and wearing a rumpled overcoat. Annie, who had worked for him in D.C., joined me to meet him along with Ken Lanphear, a reporter from WKZO radio which we had prearranged. After a brief interview train side, we drove him to the Honigman Law Firm Office in Kalamazoo (he is affiliated with the firm in Detroit), to WMUK public radio and then to the WWMT (CBS) television station for an on camera interview to support my candidacy. It was fun to watch people at each stop to do a double take when they realized who it was.

The final stop was our fundraiser, which exceeded all our expectations. The Todd conference room was packed with a diverse mix of young, old, black, white, gay, straight — you name it. Politicians get into trouble when they start taking themselves "for real." This crowd was about Carl Levin. The Todds, Caroline Ham and I were simply the beneficiaries. A gracious welcome by George Todd was followed by laudatory remarks by Senator Levin in which he cited how critical it was to flip the 6th Congressional District in order to provide a check and some balance to what the Trump administration was doing in Washington. I followed by thanking everyone and mentioning what an honor it was to have Senator Levin with us and emphasizing how everyone deserved a fair shot, but they wouldn't get such an opportunity if the Trump policies went ahead unimpeded. I also announced I was in favor of a "wall" which I found out later, almost caused Kathryn Tapper Scott to collapse – until I added, but "the only damn wall I want to build is one to keep the Asian carp out of Lake Michigan."

We hustled Senator Levin back to the Amtrak station after the event so that he could catch the train to Lansing for a late dinner with his wife. We laughed, who but Senator Levin would commute by train nowadays from Detroit to Kalamazoo to Lansing in one day.

We felt very positive as 2017 came to a close. Outreach, fundraising, staff, volunteers and endorsements all seemed to be coming together quite nicely. We felt like the campaign was firing on all cylinders. However, we had one big problem we hadn't expected. Fred Upton announced he was going to run for re-election for his House seat.

*"Eat a live frog first thing
in the morning and nothing worse will
happen to you the rest of the day."*
**Mark Twain**

## *Chapter* 11

Eli Isaguirre, my campaign manager, described his responsibilities as ranging from being "a babysitter to a social worker." Fair enough, but I perceived his role as being tantamount to a ringmaster, absent the whip, stage managing a three ring circus. In circle one you have the candidate, circle two is the paid staff and volunteers and in ring three an array of consultants, vendors and political entities.

Managing the candidate, his family and friends is the campaign version of directing the Flying Wallendas, the famous circus family known for performing high wire acts without a safety net. Not something taught in school, but rather an aspect you learn on the job. At Kellogg Company we called it "boss management." In other words, how do you keep the crazy bastard, in this case the candidate, from doing something stupid.

Candidates have lives, influences and pressures outside of the campaign. Spouses, partners, sons and daughters, family members, business interests, jobs, social obligations and generally the whole collage of life goes on while being a candidate. They impact what the candidate will or won't say or do every day and the campaign manager needs to negotiate these often conflicting demands with the focus and requirements of the campaign.

I remember Eli telling me that when he was working on the Mark Schauer for governor campaign, it was understood by staff that Mark was hell bent to get home every night which logistically presented some challenges. Obviously, considering the size of Michigan, it was not possible every night, but it did make for some long evenings.

Mark also aspired to take a Saturday or Sunday afternoon off in order to recharge his batteries and spend some time with his wife. Campaign staff would have you going at it 24/7, but they often fail to be mindful that "staffing" an event is a responsibility shared by many, but there is only one candidate. The Schauer for governor campaign had an admonition "don't kill the candidate," which was shorthand Eli and I would use in discussing what, where and when. We had a good rapport. I respected his judgement and his probity and never once second guessed his direction, counsel or management.

People management, human resources (HR) in the corporate world, may be the most vexing aspect of any organization, and campaigns are no different. Poor Eli didn't realize the size of the pooper scooper he would need to clean up after the mess resulting from the circus parade I had been running. People had positions, but as one staffer gingerly put it, "lanes were being crossed." Organization has never been my strong suit and at Kellogg I was always woeful as far as forms, processes and procedures. It was so bad that I remember my boss at Kellogg, Joe Stewart, while doing my annual performance review bellowing out, "Franklin you are an administrative nightmare." The truth hurts.

A campaign manager needs to establish structure and accountability while being the "social worker and babysitter" described by Eli. In essence, she or he is the HR department of the "business." Compensation, vacation, sick leave, child care, family issues all come under the purview of the campaign manager. People skills and the ability to communicate are critical in establishing a culture that is genuinely open, caring and inviting. The latter, which is imperative for a political campaign always looking for volunteers and an environment which I believe we did create. Whether it was Annie, Matthew, Zac or volunteers, every reference to Eli was accompanied by an encomium about the atmosphere that was present. As Reuben Glasser, one of the volunteers put it, "The office was always a fun, vibrant place to be, and I was lucky to spend a lot of my summer there." (We were lucky to have Reuben, who as a leader of the Students Against Gun Violence movement developed into a key adviser/briefer for me and the campaign on gun violence issues).

The third ring of this circus called a campaign requires the ringmaster to juggle a slew of political organizations with more acronyms than the Pentagon and campaign consultants while keeping tabs on the political prognosticators who impact your fundraising and overall political support.

Politics, like any business, has its own terminology and outside organizations you deal with and require the attention of the principals. The lexicon of terms you will hear thrown about include, inter alia (if a Republican, you can usually just substitute an R for a D to partisan entities since there is almost always a mirror image counterpart):

**FEC** – the Federal Election Commission created in 1974 as part of the Watergate Reforms. The agency is led by a six-member commission no more than three of whom can belong to the same political party. (Translation: three Democrats and three Republicans).

This is where your campaign officially begins when you file as a candidate and is where you file your campaign finance reports. The FEC is also where rules and regulations are promulgated and enforced as to what you can and can't do as a candidate.

**DNC** – the Democratic National Committee is the "company" that has run Democratic politics since its inception in 1848. (The Republican National Committee (RNC) followed shortly in 1856). Currently chaired by Tom Perez, the former secretary of labor under President Obama, the leadership also includes the chair and vice chair of each state Democratic Party and over 200 members elected by Democrats from all 50 states and territories.

"The Committee, which plans the party's presidential nominating convention and promotes the Democratic platform – the statement of core principles at the heart of our party…"

"The DNC also raises money, hires staff and co-ordinates strategy to support candidates for local, state and national office throughout the country."

**DCCC** – the "official" campaign arm of the Democrats in the House of Representatives is currently chaired by Congresswoman Cheri Bustos of Illinois. The Democratic Congressional Campaign Committee (DCCC) does everything from recruiting candidates, helping staff candidates, provides polling and political advice as well as funding. Theoretically, neutral in primaries, they have been known to "put their thumb on the scale" on behalf of certain candidates. They also run the Red to Blue Program.

**Red to Blue** – a targeting designation by the DCCC, which signals it is a priority race for resources and a race they believe presents a real opportunity to flip a seat currently Republican (Red) to Democrat (Blue). Red to Blue designation is a significant bench-mark for challengers which brings with it varying degrees of support.

**PAC** – Political Action Committees, like the FEC, date back to the Watergate reforms in 1974. They are formed by employees of companies, members of labor unions and other interest groups as a mechanism to pool their financial resources and then contribute to candidates running for political office. The amounts they can contribute are limited by law and their contributions are made public through the FEC.

**Act Blue** – Online fundraising operation and, although separate from the Democratic Party, it is only available to Democratic candidates, progressives and non-profits. Created in 2004, it has been a powerful fundraising tool that makes it easy for like-minded individuals to support candidates and causes around the country.

**EMILY'S List** – Early Money is Like Yeast was created in 1985 to support pro-choice women running for political office (The Susan B. Anthony list is the pro-life PAC counterpart). In 2018, EMILY'S List endorsed 8 women in gubernatorial races, 12 for the U.S. Senate and 64 candidates for the House of Representatives.

**GOTV** – Get Out the Vote. Campaign lingo for identifying supporters and likely supporters who then are contacted and, if need be, assisted to get to the polls to make sure they vote.

**CLF** – Congressional Leadership Fund is a PAC created in 2011, directed by the Republican leadership of the House of Representatives and is dedicated to electing GOP (Grand Old Party) members. It makes donations as well as funds staff who work in districts on GOTV and other campaign support activity.

**NGP/VAN** – Two combined private vendors, the National Geographic and Political Software with Voter Action Network, which provide a variety of functions for Democratic candidates. Some of these services include a database to track and communicate with donors, a platform from which to send fundraising emails, background on all registered voters and the ability to keep track of all voter contacts. In addition, they and other companies, provide the tools to implement and accelerate those hated robocalls. Each year an estimated 26 billion robocalls (many political) are placed and, as with other irritating means of communication, they are used because they work.

Robocalls which range in cost from only about $13 for 1,000 30-second calls are an inexpensive, quick and easy way to communicate the campaign message or denigrate your opponent.

Supposedly, cell phones are protected from this barrage of intrusive calls, but with 47% of voters not having landlines, companies promote the ability to "call cell phones and stay in compliance with FCC regulations." Finally, if you think you can find refuge in the 'Do Not Call List' you are out of luck since it does not apply to political communications.

**Vote Builder** – Software system created by NGP/VAN to track interaction with voters by storing phone contacts, door-to-door occasions and the like which can be used for GOTV.

**SMS** – Yes, Shared Message Service, or what we all call texting – peer-to-peer (P2P) is the new hot button in political communication. Like its evil twin, the annoying robocall, texting is a quick, easy and inexpensive way to make announcements, promote events, convey messages and spur voter turnout. The Democratic National Committee (DNC) in 2018 purchased 94 million cell phone numbers of registered voters and, not surprisingly, companies like Hustle for the Democrats and Opn Sesame for the Republicans have sprung up to establish databases and create SMS campaigns. Although, regarded by many as personally invasive, 90% of texts are read within three minutes of arriving literally in the hands or pockets of the targets.

In addition to orchestrating the alphabet soup of the political world and social media mentioned above, the campaign manager as the maestro of this multi-stage production needs to keep track of what the national pundits are pontificating about the race. Arguably the three most influential are Charlie Cook, Larry Sabato and Nate Silver.

Charlie Cook, a former Hill staffer, started the *Cook Political Report* in 1984 and after a series of iterations is now a team of six doing non-partisan political analysis of presidential, gubernatorial, U.S. Senate and House races. Candidates are placed in political silos of simple categories of solid, lean, likely and toss up. What silo your race is designated directly affects your ability to secure endorsements, raise funds and other support.

University of Virginia Political Science Professor Larry Sabato publishes the highly respected *Crystal Ball*. Created in 2002, it uses a similar format to the *Cook Political Report* – political silos of lean, likely, toss up and safe. Sabato is also a "talking head" on the cable TV circuit and as such his imprimatur can move the needle for a candidate.

Five hundred thirty-eight is the number of electoral votes contested in a presidential election and also the name of the political analysis provided by Nate Silver. His predictions are based on statistical models he developed in accurately predicting the state-by-state results of the 2008 presidential election. Instantly, he became a political guru. Instead of the lean, solid, likely, toss up type format, he gives the odds like a Las Vegas bookie e.g. seven in nine or 77.5% chance of winning vs. the opponent or two in nine or 22.5% chance of prevailing.

Three different analyses, one from a former Hill staffer, one from a political science professor and the last one the product of a statistician. Amazingly, all three tend to be generally consistent, and all three directly impact the political races they dissect and prognosticate.

One commodity candidates and campaign managers will get more of than they need is advice. Every campaign is subject to a plethora of unsolicited, well-meaning, often contradictory counsel, suggestions and input. As the candidate, I got it everywhere for "free" while Eli had to measure the sagacity of paid consultants.

The type of advice you get from an individual is usually a reflection of their personality and three who cared enough to contribute guidance to me on an on-going basis were very different in tone and demeanor.

Peter Battani had the F-bombing take no prisoners approach with a disheveled Steve Bannon look. Attack was his middle name. Mark Schauer, on the other hand, was the steady political pro who, after holding elected office at both the state and federal level and losing a close race for governor understood campaigns need to be like an intrepid battleship, designed to take hits, stay the course and keep fighting. Finally, there was Sheila Smith, recently married to a good friend of mine, she is somewhat soft spoken, but always thoughtful and willing to demur to national and local Democratic Party orthodoxy. Sheila's personal politics were far left on the continuum, but tempered by a practical streak garnered from a background in marketing. She always had an interesting twist or angle on policy, approaches and messaging.

We had four principle outside companies advising us, all of which reported to Eli. As a practical matter, other than a day long strategy session and a weekly call, I really didn't have that much interaction with them. My job as described once by Jason Kander, a former Missouri politician, was to be a combination telemarketer and door-to-door salesman. Management was not in the job description. That was Eli's bailiwick.

Prism Communications, particularly the firm's president B.J. Neidhardt, and to a lesser extent Peter Cari, one of the founding partners, served as our principle media and overall campaign strategy advisers. B.J. and Peter were both campaign combat veterans having done stints at the DCCC and involved with political campaigns at all levels throughout the country. Two simpatico individuals with quite different styles. B.J. was burly and brusque with a cut through the BS kind of approach. Peter was more the diplomat with a let's work this out kind of style. Their divergent yet complimentary approaches were a constructive dynamic that influenced their not always in agreement recommendations to the campaign.

Polling was handled by Jason McGrath of GBA Strategies. His firm provided the quantitative research we all think about when referring to polling (XYZ ahead 55% to 42% with 3% undecided), but more importantly helped create and/or supplement the intuition of the campaign leadership. Polling is a snapshot of a moving target. Like in hockey, you don't want to pass to where a player is, but rather where they are going to be. When I was with Kellogg Company, we would do what was then called market basket surveys. We would interview customers entering a grocery store and ask them nutritionally what they were looking to buy. Routinely the response would be a litany of the nutritional hot topics of the day – low fat, low calorie, high fiber, etc. When leaving, we would examine what they actually bought and find there was little correlation between what they professed to want and what they actually purchased. This is where a good pollster comes in. They don't just tell you what the person was thinking when they entered the store or what they bought after leaving the store. They help you understand what the person was thinking in the store. Point of purchase decision making. In politics that translates into what are the factors that will make them vote for you. McGrath was a good one.

Representative Jon Hoadley is a very sharp, progressive Democratic state legislator from Kalamazoo who won somewhat of an upset victory in his first run for elective office in 2014. He and his team implemented a masterful social media campaign to accomplish what he did. He used a Lansing based organization called Change Media Group for his digital and social media programs, and we figured if they were good enough for Hoadley they were good enough for us. We figured right. Change took charge of social media, email programs, online fundraising, list building, audience targeting and provided a ghost writer – Evelyn Maidlow – who could really turn a phrase. They were an integral part of our campaign behind the scenes and also provided a reach beyond any other component.

Targeting, timing and content are the three critical components of direct mail, and we put this aspect of the campaign in the hands of Gumbinner & Davies, a nationally recognized mail and digital advertising company. Michael Davies was the partner in charge of our account, and he came through with some superlative pieces.

It is probably no coincidence that P.T. Barnum, the founder of Barnum & Baileys and the first circus to deploy three rings, was a politician. He served two terms in the Connecticut Legislature and was also the mayor of Bridgeport. It appears as if politics might have been his inspiration for the "Greatest Show on Earth" and, quite possibly, his campaign manager made him realize that yes, one person – the ringmaster, could handle three rings simultaneously.

*"Ninety-eight percent of adults in this country are recent hard-working Americans. It's the other two percent that get all the publicity. But then, we elected them."*
**Lily Tomlin**

# *Chapter* 12

On January 3, 2018, I was snowed in, which was to portend what was coming in the next three months when I was figuratively snowed under. Approximately 284 hours of call time in January, February and March (over seven 40 hour weeks) and 135 events such as marches, rallies parades, forums, fundraisers, coffees, meet and greets, endorsement interviews and media activities. It was 90 days of getting to cross paths with hundreds of engaging, thoughtful and interesting people. It was also three months of getting those damn signatures.

Michigan requires candidates for Congress to obtain the signatures of 1,000 registered voters in the district in order to qualify for the ballot in the August primary. Unlike other states where you can pay a fee to qualify, signatures are the only way to be listed on the ballot. It does not matter what their party affiliation might be, it only requires they are registered voters in the congressional district and have not signed for another candidate. The form is pretty straightforward – name and address – but it also requires the signatory to indicate which city or township they reside in, which can be confusing and disqualifying if not correct. For example, Vicksburg is a village of approximately 3,000 people in Kalamazoo County. Ask anybody who lives there where they live and they will say Vicksburg when asked to indicate the city or township. The problem is that for purposes of ballot qualifying signatures it sort of doesn't exist. It is not a "city," and the western part of the village is in Schoolcraft Township and the eastern part is in Brady Township. Imagine the looks you get when asking for a signature and then telling people they don't live where they live.

The deadline for submitting the signatures to the secretary of state in Lansing to qualify for the August primary ballot was April 24, 2018. This means it is cold and sometimes extremely cold in Michigan when you and volunteers are stationed outside of libraries, restaurants, art shows, community gatherings – you name it – trying to secure 1,000 signatures. In fact, you need well over 1,000 signatures to provide a cushion for those disqualified for errors and confusion from places like Vicksburg (the minimum is 1,000 and the maximum allowed to be filed is 2,000).

Now this whole signature undertaking became the preoccupation of my wife Molly. One January evening I mentioned the signature requirement, which was news to her having spent her political life in Georgia where you simply pay a fee. When she asked how we planned to obtain these signatures, I casually responded, no need to worry "Eli has an app" to which she responded with a degree of agitation, "Well that app isn't going to get those signatures." (She was right; the app was a tool to verify the authenticity of the signatures.) Sensing a looming disaster, she became a dog with a bone on the project of ballot qualifying signatures. Bundled head-to-toe, she stood outside of stores, schools, community centers, libraries and was asked to leave restaurants, bars, grocery stores and a sundry of other locations. Never before has such a nice person gotten the boot from so many places. Now Molly did yeoman's work, but she was not alone in securing the 1,500 plus signatures we eventually gathered. Volunteers like Becky Baldwin, Cliff Pulley, Annika Doner and her brother Jake and others along with the campaign staff braved the weather while scouring the district for signatures. We met our target of over 1,500 signatures and would be surprised to find out in April that two candidates would fail to meet the requirement.

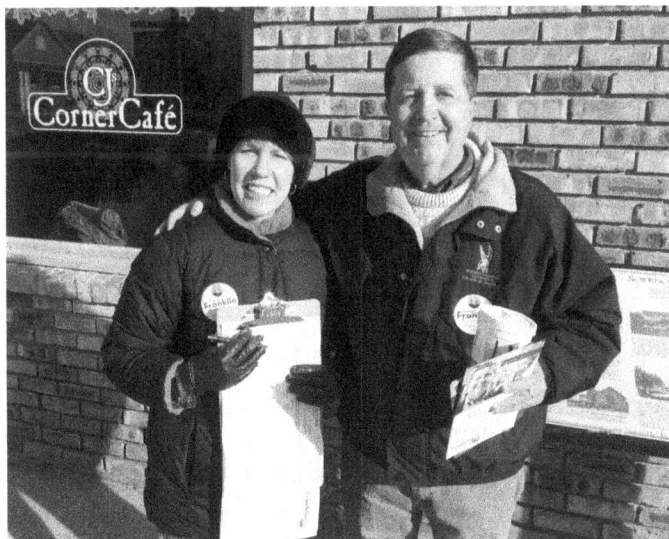

*Molly and I outside the café in Glenn soliciting those much needed signatures.*

Endorsements are important and, in a Democratic primary, organized labor still has clout. Support from them was especially important for me to establish my Democratic credentials. It was also personally important to me since the women and men of organized labor and people who just want a fair shot were what the campaign was all about. Forty percent of union households voted for Donald Trump and a lot of it had to do with a feeling that the herbal tea wing of the Democratic Party had a condescending attitude towards them and what they were all about.

Especially telling was a remonstrative admonishment I received from one of the leaders of the union building trades. He told me he was tired of hearing high-minded Democrats talk about how union workers had voted against their own interest implying that they didn't know any better. He went on to say they knew exactly what they were doing. As he explained, imagine you are a union carpenter working away on Friday afternoon with your buddy, also a union carpenter, next to you on the job site. You come to work on Monday morning and your buddy is gone and next to you is an undocumented worker who has been illegally hired with no benefits or protections, getting minimal wages in cash well below what you are making. You start thinking, am I next and then along comes this guy Trump who says you know what I am going to do? I'm going to get rid of that guy who took your buddy's job and I am going to make sure no one shows up to take yours.

Now the reality and the perception might be different, but it was enlightening to hear this version from the front lines of the culture war we have under-way. The infamous Republican operative Lee Atwater used to say, "If you want to know what the American people are thinking listen to country music and watch wrestling." I left my labor friend thinking a little country music by Aaron Tippin might help us Demo-crats better understand the blue-white collar divide.

Even though my entire professional career had been on the business side of the equation, I had good relationships with organized labor starting with my stint on Capitol Hill working with the Special Sub-committee on Labor. When the campaign first started, I was proud to get the endorsement of Rocky Marsh, former president of the Bakery, Confectionary, Tobacco Workers and Grain Millers AFL-CIO Local in Battle Creek when I was with Kellogg. In announcing his support, he stated that I was the one in management they could go to when they needed help.

My tenure on the Western Michigan University Board of Trustees further strengthened my relation-ship with organized labor as the "business guy" will-ing to help. As a result, I was gratified to secure the endorsements of the United Food and Commercial Workers (UFCW), the American Federation of State, County and Municipal Employees (AFSCME), the Operating Engineers and the Association of Postal

Supervisors. All unions that truly represent hard working men and women that keep the country going.

When you run for office a fundamental purpose must be to change people's lives for the better, but in the process of campaigning you might be fortunate to meet citizens who profoundly change you and hopefully for the better. I had such an encounter which providentially occurred on January 29, 2018, only 16 days before the horrific killing of 17 students at Marjory Stoneman Douglas High School in Parkland, Florida.

There was nothing apposite to say after meeting Rick and Martha Omillian at a coffee shop in Plainwell, Michigan. As parents, these two had been through the unimaginable, losing a beautiful and by all accounts vivacious college-age daughter in a murder suicide by her former boyfriend at Kalamazoo College. When I lost my previous wife Harriett quite unexpectedly, I would tell friends that the only thing worse would be to lose a child. Not only had they lost a child, but in circumstances which would cause most of us to curl up permanently in the fetal position. Not these two. They were activists committed to educating the public and proposing policy that addressed the interrelationship of gun violence, suicide and violence against women. My hour long coffee with them has had a lasting impact on me. Such that, post-election, I now am with a community group trying to establish a domestic violence court to prevent violence by attacking the root causes.

Prior to meeting the Omillians and the Parkview shooting, I really didn't have strong views on gun control and/or gun violence. Whatever position I took in this area of debate would not cause me to resile from where I had been. It wasn't front and center for me, but after that coffee in Plainwell and Parkland it was and is now.

In law school, I had studied the Second Amendment and now found myself surprisingly quoting one of the most conservative justices on the Supreme Court, Antonin Scalia:

*"Like most rights, the right secured by the Second Amendment is not unlimited..." it is "not a right to keep and carry any weapon whatsoever in any manner whatsoever and for whatever purpose."*

You can't tote a bazooka down main street, and people that are a danger to themselves and others should not be allowed to purchase or own firearms. Now how do you accomplish this as a matter of public policy?

On February 25, post-Parkland, I was asked to attend a community anti-gun violence gathering at the home of Katie and Jeff Stryker in Kalamazoo. They were appalled by what had happened and hoped to initiate a conversation that would result in meaningful change. There was a tremendous turnout, which packed the house and made us all quite sanguine that this time after the horrendous event in Florida, significant, impactful modifications in societal thinking and public policy could be effectuated. My remarks followed Representative Jon Hoadley and County Commissioner Kevin Wordelman, both serious, successful, practical and respected elected officials. Neither subject to hackneyed slogans, but real solutions. In my tutorial with the Omillians a few weeks previous, I had learned about the so called "red flag" provision being advocated and thought it made imminent sense while passing legal muster and decided to make it part of my approach to preventing gun violence. The red flag provision struck me as something practical and legislatively doable, NRA or no NRA. Simply put, the red flag approach would, as I like to put it, allow judges to be judges. Most of the time when you had a Columbine, Sandy Hook or Parkland shooting, people knew something was wrong with the perpetrator beforehand. Friends, schoolmates, relatives, social media contacts, law enforcement realized/noticed that something wasn't right, and a red flag provision would allow them to go before a judge ("standing" in legalese) who with probable cause could prevent that individual from buying, owning or possessing a gun. An approach I believe Justice Scalia would affirm.

I discovered a not very well kept secret while campaigning in African American neighborhoods and attending predominantly black churches. There is a strong conservative streak in that constituency but, unlike some evangelicals who wear religion on their sleeves, these folks have it residing in their hearts where it counts.

Whether it was Lily of the Valley congregation in Covert under Pastor Daryl Williams, Galilee Baptist in Kalamazoo with Dr. Michael Scott, or Pilgrim Rest Baptist in Benton Harbor officiated by Pastor Emery Varrie, there was an energy and a sense of community unlike any other church service I have attended. Praising the Lord is first and foremost, but Sunday service is so much more. They have an esprit de corps which is infectious, abetted by music which is magnificent. Each of these churches are located in spots where there are tough times outside of those doors, but you would never know from the welcoming attitude Molly, Annie and I would receive those Sunday mornings. Upbeat, positive and embracing were the common denominators within each congregation which made attending church a true joy.

Politically, the predominately African American churches shared a perspective at odds with Democratic Party orthodoxy in that they uniformly opposed legalization of marijuana which was on the ballot. I favored the ballot proposal, but must admit their opposition made me think twice. The presence of illegal drugs has ravished their communities, and we are talking about people who can't afford thousands of dollars to send loved ones to rehab like people in the wealthier suburbs do. They are on the front lines of the drug war, which made me think as such, they might know more about what is going on in the streets than those of us in more privileged positions.

Another issue which is problematic in black churches is LGBTQ rights – a movement I strongly support. I believe gay rights are the civil rights issue of our era. Matthew Craig of the campaign staff taught me a succinct way to frame the issue.

*"It is wonderful that gay marriage is now legal. Sure, gays can get married on Sunday, but they also can get fired on Monday and evicted on Tuesday."*

It isn't right that this type of discrimination is allowed in 2018. My perception of predominantly African American churches is that they are in a "don't ask, don't tell" phase. The evolution of candidate Obama's support for civil unions to President Obama's support for gay marriage is a change of heart which I believe will be a catalyst for a similar metamorphosis in the attitude of majority African American churches. Hopefully accompanied by a similar change of heart in the minds and souls of conservative Republicans as was the case with the late Senator Barry Goldwater (R-AZ) who, when asked about gays in the military responded, "I don't care who they sleep with, I want to know if they can shoot straight." By the way, he also notably suggested that "every good Christian should line up and kick Jerry Falwell's (leader of the evangelical movement) ass."

I was proud to earn the endorsement of many of the black clergy. These men and women of the cloth fight the daily struggles of their flock and deserve our kudos for doing so.

If you ever meet Gwen Hooker and/or Mattie Jordan-Woods, you will never forget them. They are change agents. Two African American women with intrepid spirits who fight the odds every day.

I met Gwen, who was vice president of membership of the Kalamazoo Chapter of the National Association for the Advancement of Colored People (NAACP) at the annual spring fundraiser for Representative Jon Hoadley. She was staffing a promotional table for the NAACP and I stopped by to introduce myself. In the course of informal chit-chat, I mentioned that my family had an unusual involvement in the civil rights movement in that Rosa Parks' bus, was "my father's bus." Not literally, but the company he worked for, National City Lines, owned the Montgomery City Lines along with other bus companies around the country.

*Direct Mail Piece*

When Rosa Parks courageously refused to give up her seat to a white man, a bus boycott ensued; my father was dispatched to negotiate and resolve the situation with Dr. Martin Luther King. During the heated atmosphere of the Montgomery bus boycott, the chair of the Alabama Public Service Commission who was also the head of the White Citizen's Council (aka Ku Klux Klan) ordered my father to re-segregate the buses. My father in turn wrote him back and in polite legalese told him to go shove it.

Subsequent to Montgomery, my father negotiated with Dr. King numerous times in multiple cities involving civil rights and public access. He had a great deal of respect for Dr. King, who he found to be an honorable man willing to work towards a resolution of whatever the issue was at hand.

Gwen and I agreed to have a follow-up on our conversation at her NAACP office in the Northside of Kalamazoo. When we got together, she off handedly asked where I was coming from, to which I responded a lunch with civic leaders organized by Judge Schma, followed by my question to her, "Do you know him?" I will never forget her response, "He saved my life." Quite a powerful statement which stopped me for a moment. "What do you mean he saved your life?"

Gwen was a product of the drug court and it was Judge Schma, local founder and national leader of the drug court movement, who had turned her life around. As she recounted, he was one of the few people who had faith in her, and she was hell bent on returning his belief in her by giving back to those less fortunate and living on the fringes. If someone is getting out of prison with nowhere to go, they can call Gwen and she will help. If a child is getting getting bullied at school, Gwen has a program to stop that. She has organized an alphabet soup of coalitions, associations and causes to benefit the most exposed and unprotected in our society. Although her resources are meager, her impact is fecund.

Mattie Jordan-Woods is a five foot (maybe) dynamo and right out of the box in our first discussion gave me an economics lecture on what she was looking for on behalf of the predominately African American Northside of Kalamazoo. As the executive director of the Northside Association for Community Development (NACD), she means business literally and figuratively. We don't just want government gifts or grants was her reproach to the notion that her focus was government largesse. Quite the contrary, she reminded me of former pro football player, congressman and vice presidential candidate Jack Kemp, who espoused the creation of enterprise zones as the way out of poverty. Mattie is quick to tell you that what she wants is, "Investment, business and jobs."

The entrepreneurial spirit sometimes just needs a little nurturing, and Mattie decided to create such a catalyst by instituting a free 10-week course on how to start a business. The course was taught by accomplished professionals with expertise in law, accounting and other fields necessary to create a new business. Annie and I attended the first night and you couldn't help but be impressed. Fifty or so wannabe business owners of very modest means pulling themselves up by their own bootstraps.

Upon graduation from the course, the idea was to help them get micro loans to buy the lawnmower, hair clippers, vacuum cleaner or whatever else that might be needed to get the enterprise up and running. Great in theory, but with one major hiccup. Most of those entrepreneurs working so hard to advance themselves did not qualify for a loan of any size. I thought to myself can't somebody give these folks a break? As a regional board member of Chemical Bank, I took the case to Perry Wolfe, community president of the bank. Now you won't find a more caring and community involved banker than Perry. His problem, however, was that banks cannot legally make loans to unqualified applicants, nor should they, in order to maintain the integrity and stability of the banking system. He agreed that this was a worthy cause and came up with the clever idea of having the bank, as part of its community responsibilities, make a grant to NACD which then could become the lending institution. Bingo. Chemical Bank made a $5,000 grant which in turn will generate economic activity in the Northside. Real companies, real jobs, real chance. Jack Kemp would be proud.

Campaigning will often help you punch through the fog of what you think and provide some clarity. In the case of Mattie and Gwen, the new-found lucidity on my part actually caused me to become quite infuriated. So little investment could go so far in the hardscrabble parts of towns, yet it never really happens. Righteous indignation would declare it a handout and antithetical to the free market system. Now if you are a billionaire owner of a pro sports team, no problem. In 2000, the government chipped in a paltry $175 million to build the "factory" for the Illitch family business in Detroit which is known as Comerica Park, i.e. Tiger Stadium. In 2002, the government anted up roughly $145 million to help the Ford family create a new home for the Detroit Lions in a city that needs a lot more than a new football stadium. Finally, take a look at the last two Super Bowls to see the apogee of corporate welfare. In 2018, the big game was held in Minneapolis, where the Minnesota Vikings team owner Zygi Wilf with a net worth of $5.3 billion had the assistance of taxpayer dollars to the tune of $498 million, so that he would have a new playpen.

Likewise, in Atlanta in 2019 where another billionaire was in need of help. In this case, Arthur Blank, with a net worth of approximately $4.7 billion and owner of the Atlanta Falcons and also the Atlanta United Pro Soccer Club, received government assistance of $700 million so that people watching his two clubs would be comfortable and dry in Mercedes-Benz Stadium with its retractable roof. Considering that

$700 million would have allowed the city with a crime problem to have hired an estimated 300 police officers for 30 years, creating the commodious environs of Mercedes-Benz Stadium must have been very important. I am not against economic incentives, but favor only those that, after a cost benefit analysis, actually do benefit the community. In the case of sports stadiums, proponents pitch the benefits while conveniently ignoring the cost of neglected other activities.

When I was with Kellogg Company, I was asked one time by a senior officer if I could get a state to flat out build us a factory. I laughed at the suggestion thinking how ludicrous it would be, but I am not laughing anymore. Spending hundreds of millions of dollars to build "factories" for the Illitch's, Ford's, Wilf's and Blank's is routinely done with minimal economic justification and little, if any, long-term meaningful job creation. They get the money because they have the political clout to get the money. If you took a smidgen of that money and built a real factory for a startup company, say a company with a new food product being sourced somewhere else and put it in an economically disadvantaged area, you could have a real factory, making a real product, employing denizens of the neighborhood on a year round basis. By capitalizing on some variation of the job tax credit under which a company financially benefits dollar for dollar equal to taxes created by new wages, you create a win-win. It translates into new jobs and revitalized neighborhoods. In so doing, you might just give the constituencies of Mattie and Gwen an opportunity for a new life.

The first quarter of 2018 was chockablock full of fundraisers, forums, meet and greets and people offering valuable help. Rick Halpert, an accomplished trial lawyer, coached me on the art of persuasion; Vicki Eichstaedt who is tech savvy, helped pump up our social media; Shannon Sykes-Nehring, a Kalamazoo city commissioner, graciously provided input on social issues (she ended up endorsing David Benac); Ken Peterson, a Vietnam War veteran, advised on military matters; and Brian Smith, a wonderful artist and self-proclaimed far-left advocate, was a terrific sounding board.

The meet and greets, which I always enjoyed continued at an accelerated pace by virtue of a ripple effect. One would beget another. Dan and Carol McGlinn hosted one evening and with Carol, the president of the Kalamazoo Public School Board of Education, it had an educational tilt and allowed me to meet Patti Sholler-Barber, also a member of the Board of Education who in turn hosted a get together for me. Donna and Rob Keller had a smashing event with a large contingent of the Kalamazoo health network including Frank Sardone, president and CEO of Bronson Hospital and his wife Susan Fall. Toni and Dave Buskirk, Ed and Doreen Thomas, Derm Putnam and Sheila Smith, Rem Cabrera and Chris Schram were some of the people who kindly opened their homes to our campaign. Now they weren't always a resounding success and when they fell a little short, I kept in mind my friend Martin O'Malley, former governor of Maryland, who when running for president of the United States in 2016 had an event in Iowa where only one person showed up. Peter Battani and Vicki Ketner hosted an evening attended by three neighbors, Troy and Michele Serlin-Zukowki and their daughter Julia. God bless 'em. This was topped, however, by a meet and greet one night in Three Oaks which was about an hour or so drive. No one was there other than the host. He finally went outside and corralled four people walking down Main Street. Nice people, but one problem. They were all from Indiana. As I learned over the course of the campaign, some things you just have to take in stride.

Forums continued at a steady pace with the six of us (seven for a short while) and following the similar format. Opening statement, round robin of questions and short closing. The topics and emphasis would change somewhat with the news cycle, e.g. post-Parkland, more discussion on gun violence (Matt Longjohn claimed his life had been threatened by the NRA), but mostly it was staying the course with the campaign's core message. Rich Eicholz's clean energy jobs; Paul Clement's climate change; David Benac's campaign finance reform (he had a great line declaring elections should not be an auction); Eponine Garrod's progressive causes; Matt Longjohn's, as a doctor designated by President Obama as one of the top 100 health innovators in the country. (Interestingly, regarding the top 100 designation, we never could find where and when this occurred. Maybe it did and we just couldn't find it, but later in the general election what didn't occur struck me as the political variation of Sherlock Holmes and the dog that didn't bark, more on that later.) I stuck with my fair shot mantra.

Not all the forums involved all the candidates and were naturally neutral. One evening I was given the opportunity to appear before ProKzoo at an event at the Kalamazoo Public Library. ProKzoo and my candidacy shared one critical element in common in that both were a result of Donald Trump being elected president. Starting with a post-election coffee shop meeting with six friends, it quickly grew into an organization with 2,000 members, 1,000 of whom were actively involved "around progressive values" aimed at implementing "direct and collective action." I knew there would be few likely supporters in the room, but they are thoughtful and engaged activists and, if you want the job, you better be willing to expose and defend your views in front of any and all. As expected, there were tough questions and I actually enjoyed taking them head on which I must have done in some fashion since upon leaving Bill Farmer, a vocal conscientious labor activist, commented to me in the hall, "You sure got balls." This remark was preceded by other words that may have been negative or positive, but I just can't remember. Regardless, his statement I considered as a plus. Win or lose, I wanted to be known as a straight shooter.

It also was the period in which a question regarding Democratic Party political support became routine

and eventually became known as the "George" question – as in me. The question was a straightforward,
"Will you support whoever is the eventual nominee?"
Since my mission was to have someone who would
vote for a Democratic speaker, my simple response
was, "Yes." Eponine Garrod, to her candid credit, was
a no if it was me. Rich Eicholz, like me, was a simple
yes. Matt Longjohn would vote for me, but not work
or actively support me, and Paul Clements and David
Benac had some version of that theme. Things were
getting interesting.

*"I am a man of fixed and unbending principles, the first of which is to be flexible at all times."*

**Senator Everett Dirksen**

## Chapter 13

April 1, 2018 – four months and seven days until the primary election and a lot of the same and a lot of the new. The next three months would mean putting the pedal to the metal. Two hundred fifty-three hours of call time, 122 events, additional staff, a bevy of interns, fundraisers, parades, senior citizen centers, coffees and the "lights, cameras, action" of making TV commercials.

Field organizers are the front line troops of a campaign. They recruit, train and direct volunteers to do the door knocking, bell ringing, phone banking and texting of a campaign with an eye toward absentee voters and Get Out the Vote (GOTV) on Election Day. You need a certain verve to be a political field organizer and we brought on three new staffers with just that to augment and fill out what Matthew Craig and Annie had started.

There is a network of 20/30-year-old campaign personnel that literally move about the country campaign-to-campaign practicing their craft. Eli tapped into this network to bring on Charlie Beal, Lincoln Wang and Amanda Lammon. Three very different personalities with a common trait of indefatigability. Charlie, always positive, would become field director; Lincoln, a steady-as-she-goes type, would be the organizer in vote rich and difficult to navigate Berrien County; and Amanda, who was a real street fighter, would tough it out in very red St. Joseph and Cass counties; while Matthew would continue to be in charge of the mother lode, Kalamazoo; and Anne would ride herd over VanBuren and Allegan counties.

Volunteers, especially younger ones, are what make a campaign fun. No disrespect to my fellow older citizens, but youth in the headquarters provides a dynamic that is irreplaceable. Ava Keller, Emma Alzner, Brady Broderick, Jonah Pilnick, Reuben Glaser, Tyler Krasny, Donovan Williams, Logan Peters and others were in and out routinely making calls, texting, going door to door and doing the "stuff" of campaigns. Smart, fun and engaged, they are the ones that made if feel like a full-fledged campaign.

During April, May and June, the campaign took on a new tempo created by the arrival of the new field team. A cadre of volunteers and springtime. The latter being a strong inducement for more door to door. I became convinced during this period that the indomitable Annie had never seen a door she didn't want to knock on. Portage, Benton Harbor, South Haven – you name it – we would strike out with addresses and names of likely Democratic voters on either ol' fashion clipboards or iPads, and I would often be reprimanded by Annie, aka "Mother Superior," for going "rogue" which meant I was stopping and talking with people not on the list. Sure was more fun that way.

Most of my door to door was with Annie, sometimes Charlie, and once in a while with an elected official or party activist. Part of going door to door is carrying "lit" (short for literature, as in handouts) for other candidates such as Joey Andrews for state representative, Garnet Lewis for state Senate and Alberta Griffin for state representative when walking areas in their respective districts. One afternoon I walked an area near Kalamazoo College with County Commissioner Tracy Hall. It was fun since we both went rogue, but more importantly, I got to know a person who is the embodiment of someone in politics for all the right reasons. A self-effacing, thoughtful individual, Tracy is trying to make where she lives a little bit better for everyone. Tracy is everything right about those who run and hold elected office.

Whether it was with Annie, Charlie, Tracy or whomever, it was clear that door to door is where you find out whether you really ought to be running for office. Most people are surprisingly welcoming and willing to talk. (Not always. Peter Battani, going door to door for me, was asked by a woman in a lawn chair for some of my literature. She looked at it, ripped it up and tossed it into the dumpster announcing, "We don't vote for communists in this house." We put her down as undecided.) You see where people live and hear their concerns from the economically disadvantaged front porches of Benton Harbor to the wealthy enclaves of Portage. My take was that people are all really kind of the same. They want a decent job with fair wages, good schools, a safe environment in which they are treated with dignity and opportunity for their kids. Whether poor, rich, black, white, gay or straight, the aspirations are all about the same. It confirmed in me all that is encapsulated in getting a fair shot.

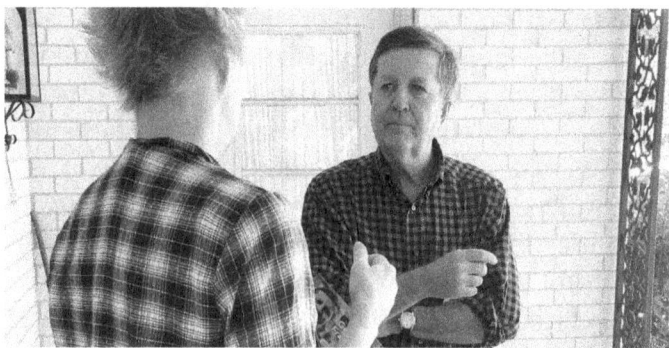

*Learning about issues of concern while knocking on doors in Portage.*

*Sort of like the postal service – rain or shine, door to door with my lit.*

Meet and greets blossomed with the springtime weather. People like Patti Sholler-Barber, Jim Perry and Charlie Adams and Toy True (neat lady with a great name) opened their homes and backyards for neighborhood gatherings.

Parades also coincide with the season, and Molly and I armed with a Franklin for Congress banner and volunteers equipped with buckets of candy worked a slew of them.

*Molly and I stepping out in another parade*

Festivals also abound like Kalamazoo Pride organized by Outfront on behalf of the LGBTQ community. It is quite the event with sponsors like Kellogg Company, Stryker, PNC Bank and smaller entities like our campaign supporting the two-day festival. Matthew and I worked the vendor tents one afternoon where I took from a jar what I thought was beef jerky and after taking a large bite was informed it was a dog treat. Oh well, we all got a laugh out of that and after remembering that one time George H. W. Bush while campaigning for president tried to shake the hand of a mannequin, I decided that a dog treat didn't taste all that bad.

Forums were becoming quite routine and began to remind me of a NASCAR race where, although no one admits it, most are in attendance to witness a wreck. In this case, a political wreck where one gaffe can derail a campaign. There was one very significant change, however, in that after April 24 what had been a field of six candidates was now whittled down to four since, very unexpectedly, Paul Clements and Eponine Garrod did not file enough signatures to qualify for the ballot.

Eli and I went to the secretary of state office in Lansing on April 23 to formally file our 1,500 plus signatures. It is quite a scene as candidates for governor, U.S. Senate, U.S. Congress and the state legislature, Republican and Democrat, file in bakery line style, sit with a Bureau of Elections staff member to log in their petitions and have them stamped with the time and date. Each candidate then struts outside hoping to get some free media with a local TV station and/or newspaper.

All six of us filed our petitions in a timely fashion, but what happened to Paul Clements and Eponine Garrod was illustrative of the vagaries of politics and campaigns. Eponine Garrod filed 1,019 signatures which as one newspaper put it, left "little breathing room" and with such little margin for error drew the attention of the staff of the secretary of state. The probability of having over 20 with material error is quite high and sure enough 45 were disqualified, leaving her with only 974 valid signatures, 26 short of 1,000. She was off the ballot and out of the running.

Paul Clements had a few more twists and turns and a tad bit of political intrigue with his situation. He filed 1,346 signatures which upon initial review it was adjudged that 1,145 qualified. Nice cushion in his numbers. So far so good. Out of the blue, at least to us, Andrew Davis, a former congressional candidate and Matt Longjohn supporter filed a formal challenge to the Paul Clements' petitions resulting in a further review and disqualification of another 157 signatures. Paul Clements was now nine short of 1,000 and deemed ineligible for the ballot. What a heartbreaker. All that time, money and effort to come up nine short. Understandably, he went to the U.S. District Court seeking relief, arguing that the Michigan election law had an inherent "fatal defect" that adversely affected his and the voter's rights. His lawyers also argued that because voters flunked a "geography test" by checking the wrong city or township box should not be sufficient to disqualifying him. Neither argument proved persuasive. U.S. District Court Judge Robert Jonker determined, "The potential for confusion did not prevent four other Democratic candidates from qualifying for the ballot with the required signatures." "Mr. Clements has failed to make a convincing showing that the court should re-write state election rules in the middle of the game."

I had mixed emotions about both candidates being disqualified, but especially Paul Clements. I know the rules are the rules, but falling nine short after twice being a nominee was in plain language "chicken shit" and I called him and told him exactly that. Politically, we always believed, and in hindsight I still do, that a crowded field was to my advantage, but substantively, as opposed to politically, Paul Clements and Eponine Garrod should have been on the ballot. They were real candidates with platforms, a significant cadre of supporters and God knows they had both worked hard campaigning. I understand the premise behind the petition requirement, but maybe allowing candidates to simply pay a fee, like many states in lieu of petitions, while keeping signatures as a cost-free avenue to access the ballot might eliminate what I thought was an unfair outcome in the 6th Congressional District of Michigan primary.

The bane of every congressional candidate is fundraising. I heard one candidate from another state describe it as "soul sucking." Whatever derogatory description you want to put with it does not negate the need to do it if you plan to communicate with 700,000 plus people over six counties.

Like many of the candidates, I decided to head to Washington, D.C. to raise some funds and no, not from lobbyists per se, but from old friends some of whom used to be lobbyists or Capitol Hill staffers. It was fun getting reconnected.

Don Kaniewski was a college roommate and fellow go-fer with Representative Frank Thompson (D-NJ). Don went on to become the director of legislative affairs for the Laborers' International Union of North America and as such was well-connected and well-respected in organized labor. As Eli commented one time, "Everybody in organized labor knows this guy." Tom Jolly is a Michigan guy who worked for Congressman Bill Ford (D-MI) as his counsel and who went on to become a very successful lawyer/lobbyist, especially close with Senator Ted Kennedy. Don and Tom, two great guys with the same, "We don't know why you are doing this, but we will support you anyways" attitude. Faye Padgett, aka 'Big Red' who I used to run errands for in the Thompson congressional office, rousted up old contacts and acquaintances, and Micah Green who I knew in my young lawyer days and is now a prominent D.C. lawyer stepped up to the plate. Headlining the event were two Democratic Party stalwarts, former governor and presidential candidate Martin O'Malley of Maryland and Dave Bonior, a former congressman from Michigan, Democratic whip of the House and political pioneer in the environmental movement. The event was very successful and it was an honor to have two notables like Martin O'Malley and Dave Bonior gathered with a group of dear friends I had not seen in a while.

Time is a limited and valuable commodity in campaigns, meaning everyday must be chockablock with activity, and a day spent in D.C. before the fundraiser was no different. Eli arranged for us to meet with Congresswoman Cheri Bustos (D-IL) who had become somewhat of a guru for Midwest Democrats after defeating a Republican incumbent in 2012 and becoming the only Democrat in the House of Representatives in Illinois not from the Chicago area. She has since become the new chair of the Democratic Congressional Campaign Committee (DCCC). The meeting with her and her chief of staff was, as expected, a general get acquainted session. We hoped we were laying the groundwork for support in a general election effort.

Per my suggestion, we also stopped by to see Congressman Jim Cooper (D-TN) with whom I had become political friends during my years in Washington. Jim is a Rhodes Scholar, Harvard Law graduate and a leader of the Blue Dog Coalition (fiscally responsible centrist Democrats). He is considered one of the most bipartisan members of Congress and one of the few members left,

Republican or Democrat, perspicacious enough to recognize the danger of a cascading federal debt and not simply give lip service to the issue like many of his colleagues in both parties. Donald Trump as a candidate breezily promised to eliminate the national debt, which is now a staggering $22 trillion. The only problem with that promise is that after two years of the Trump administration and complete Republican control it is burgeoning at a rate of $1 trillion per year and is expected to be $38 trillion in 2029. When it comes to fiscal responsibility, Jim Cooper is one of the few members willing to call a spade a spade.

It was fun to get together with Jim and share some old stories. I appreciated his support and sage counsel.

Finally, if you think a day away from the congressional district is a day away from call time, think again. Eli had arranged some time for us at the call time room at the Democratic National Committee headquarters a couple of blocks down from the House of Representatives office buildings. List in hand, we joined others upstairs in a room filled with partitioned cubicles to dial for dollars. Incumbents, challengers, neophytes and experienced pros sardined in a room soliciting what former California Speaker Jesse Unruh categorized as the "mothers milk of politics" – campaign contributions.

Back in the 6th Congressional District of Michigan, two people from my past really stepped up and made a difference on my behalf. Julie Fletcher Wolpe and Jim Margolis. Julie the widow of former Congressman Howard Wolpe and Jim, his former chief of staff.

Howard Wolpe was the congressman from what was then the 3rd Congressional District of Michigan, which combined Kalamazoo and Battle Creek until they were split into different congressional districts during the redistricting in 1992. This new configuration resulted in Howard (a resident of Kalamazoo) being pitted against the incumbent Republican Fred Upton in the 6th Congressional District, should he decide to run. He opted not to run after determining that the demographics of his new district was not winnable for a Democrat. (There is still a lingering misconception that Howard, a Western Michigan University professor, was able to prevail in a district that is now the 6th Congressional District, which is way off the mark. It was quite the opposite). Howard, who died in 2011, is justifiably much revered in Michigan Democratic circles and I was quite proud to have the support of Julie. When I was the Kellogg lobbyist, Howard represented Battle Creek where Kellogg is headquartered and as a result, we dealt with many contentious issues, not the least of which was American companies doing business in South Africa during apartheid. Howard chaired the Africa Subcommittee of the Committee on Foreign Affairs and was a nationally recognized leader, if not the leader of the worldwide anti-apartheid movement calling for companies to divest of all holdings in South Africa. Kellogg was a signatory of the Sullivan Code with a plant in Springs, South Africa. Kellogg and Howard shared a commitment to eliminate apartheid, but the rub was how best to accomplish this shared objective. To say there was some friction would be quite the understatement and part of my job became how to prevent all-out war between the local congressman and his largest constituent/employer. Somehow we were able to prevent both sides from entering into a phase of mutual destruction and in so doing, Julie with I think some hyperbole, credited me with "helping Howard keep his seat." Regardless of how much credit I deserved, having her imprimatur meant a lot and carried great weight with a wide swath of Democrats.

Jim Margolis is a two-fer in the political world of Southwest Michigan. Son of Dr. Fred Margolis, a beloved pediatrician in Kalamazoo, he helped engineer Howard Wolpe's first successful election to Congress and is now one of the most respected and sought after Democratic political/media advisers in D.C. So much so, that he has become an inductee into the American Association of Political Consultants Hall of Fame. His induction was met with accolades from such luminaries as Speaker Nancy Pelosi, former Majority Leader Harry Reid, Senator Mark Warner and David Axelrod. I say two-fer in that not only does he have local recognition, but also national having served as one of the half dozen or so key advisers in both of President Obama's runs for the White House. His role was so critical that David Axelrod tells the story of recruiting Jim to join the Obama campaign imploring him to "just come to

Chicago to meet this guy" which he did and that turned out to be a good day for Jim and President Obama.

Jim has a summer home in Northern Michigan and agreed to be the guest of honor for me at a fundraiser in Kalamazoo. It was magnanimous of him doing so with the constraints on his time and especially considering I had not hired his firm to handle my campaign. It was a beautiful summer evening well attended by a lot of folks who started the conversation with, "I knew your parents." I believe Jim in Kalamazoo for this event would end up being the highest-level Obama "person" campaigning in the 6th Congressional District in either the primary or general election.

One fun aside to Jim being in Kalamazoo to campaign for me was taking him by the house in town where he grew up. Conveniently, the house is now owned by Joe Hawver, a highly-respected Assistant Prosecutor who I had gotten to know during the campaign. Touring his boyhood home was a lot of fun and especially when he identified the piano in the living room as the same one that was there when he was a kid.

Shooting commercials was an experience. I am not sure what I really expected when I arrived early that Sunday morning at the Walnut & Park Cafe, but it was more than I anticipated. A Hollywood scene of makeup artists, lights, boom mics, extras and a camera crew scurrying about. This was big time and it was going to be a long and expensive ($25,000 - $30,000) day to shoot three commercials entitled "Barely Knew," "Involved" and "Promise." It would involve four different locations, numerous changes of clothes and a lot of good-spirited volunteers as extras all of whom I promised movie stardom.

Eli had scoped out and made arrangements for the four venues in advance. Walnut & Park agreed to the early morning shoot with the assurance we would buy a lot of coffee and we were good to our word. Following the coffee shop, our entourage with cars, trucks and trailers headed over to the Moses L. Walker Building of the Family Health Center, courtesy of Mr. Walker. Moses has been a longtime Kalamazoo health/hospital executive who I knew through years of civic and political engagement. The building, named in his honor, had the hospital look and feel we needed for our health care ad.

The final two sites were in a quintessential Midwest neighborhood at the homes of Dan and Carol McGlinn and their neighbor Elena Campos. They generously vacated their homes for most of a day and allowed our crew to move furniture, pictures, rearrange book shelves, knick-knacks and generally take over their homes. The tree lined street and the houses with porches and American flags flapping in the breeze reminded me of a setting that could have been used in filming the iconic Ronald Reagan commercial "Morning in America."

The first ad "Barely Knew" was about health care and was personally the most sensitive to Molly and me. The scene called for me to be casually dressed, half sitting on a window sill within a small alcove, looking into the camera and describing how my deceased wife Harriett had gone from what we thought was perfect health to dying from cancer in seven days; no one needed to tell me about the importance of health care. Molly and I had talked about how we felt doing this and she was okay with it. As she said, it was reality, it had happened and when you run for office people deserve to know who you are and what you are all about. Originally, B.J. and the Prism Group wanted to include a picture of Harriett in the scene which both Molly and I nixed as to unsettling. I told B.J., "I am not going there," and he understood with no push-back. Filming it was another issue. It was difficult. I had a script, but was halting in delivery. Finally, Peter Cari said, in essence, just throw the script away and just say it which turned out to be great advice. I realized it was too personal to use someone else's words, so I just said it. As a result, it came out naturally and since it was a powerful story it resulted in an ad that was impactful.

Making "Involved" was fun since we filmed it with my two daughters both of whom are in their early 30's. Christy flew in from Los Angeles, met her sister Katy in Chicago and drove over for the day. The scene was the two of them seated at a kitchen counter holding a photo of the three of us when they were six and seven. Together they described how I had always encouraged them to get involved and make a difference. Don't sit on the sidelines and watch the world go by. The camera then focused on a supposed text from me on Christy's phone with her quipping, "And he still does." They then go on to say how I will always stand up to Donald Trump on behalf of equal pay for women, Planned Parenthood and women's rights.

The final piece called "Promise" had me harking back to when my father was in WWII and the values he instilled in me from the "Greatest Generation." Using his military pictures as a backdrop in the beginning, then me on a porch with the neighbor's American flag over my shoulder I recite how he taught me a "deal was a deal" and a promise is to be kept. I then transition into how Medicare and Social Security programs are something seniors have paid for and are commitments that must be honored.

Creating TV advertising is an expensive under-taking and airing them is really expensive. The cost is calculated by a formula called the gross rating points which, when translated into layman's terms, means the viewership of the station, how much repetition the ad will get and what that will result in as far as impressions to the target audience. Ideally, in our case, we would have the 35 and over crowd see the ad 10 times in a week, which means in the Grand Rapids – Kalamazoo market we would need to write $50,000 to $60,000 checks and a little bit less for South Bend, Indiana, TV that covered the southern part of the district. By the way, you need to pay in advance, no credit for campaigns.

You may be thinking why TV in this age of social media. If my experience is a true reflection that screen in the living room is still the big guerilla. Once our ads started appearing there was an immediate response. Total strangers would stop me in grocery stores, parking lots or walking down the street and say, "Aren't you the guy with the daughters," or "So sorry to hear about your wife." I was in their living rooms telling my story and there was an instant connection.

The #Me Too Movement and accompanying discussion on sexual harassment and sexual assault was very much in the forefront in early summer of 2018. Numerous business leaders, especially in the movie industry, were being called to task for behavior that was totally unacceptable. In this environment, I attended the YWCA Women of Achievement dinner recognizing truly notable women in the region for all that they had accomplished. It was an inspiring evening and when leaving I ran into Tim Light. Tim is without question one of the most respected, philanthropic and civic-minded individuals in Kalamazoo. A noted Chinese scholar, he had been provost of Western Michigan University when I was a trustee and he and I had forged a friendship during that period. "Do you remember what you did on the sexual harassment issue when you were on the board?" he asked me. "I'm not sure what you mean," I responded. He then went on to remind me of my action well before anyone had heard of the #Me Too Movement. The then president of the university, Diether Haenicke, had negotiated with the faculty a new sexual harassment policy which he presented to the Board of Trustees in a closed session. Also in the session was Tim the provost; Bob Beam, CFO of the university; Betty Kocher, the board secretary and Carol Hustoles, the general counsel. Diether's proposal was, "Sexual harrassment MAY be grounds for dismissal." Tim reminded me that I immediately spoke up and said that wasn't good enough. Maybe it was being the father of two daughters or maybe it's the lawyer in me, but I proposed we take it a step further. My proposal was that the language should read, "Sexual harassment SHALL be cause for dismissal." Diether and the Board agreed.

The end of June had us looking at 48 days until the election. We felt pretty good, but of course feeling any different would be about as useful as an ashtray on a motorcycle. We knew the next month we would be attacked, i.e. someone would go negative on us. We were surprised by whom and for what.

Carl Sandburg the famous poet is known to have recommended:

> *"If the facts are against you, argue the law.*
> *If the law is against you, argue the facts.*
> *If the law and the facts are against you,*
> *pound the table and yell like hell."*

Possibly, Eponine Garrod was a faithful of Carl Sandburg and following his direction, or maybe she thought she would become the political poet laureate of Michigan. Regardless of her motivations the last month or so would be a wild ride.

*"Vote for you?*
*Why I'd rather vote for the devil."*
**Constituent**

*"I understand, but in case your friend is not*
*running, may I count on your support?"*
**Winston Churchill**

# Chapter 14

Dynamic, tough, smart. Jennifer Granholm, the first female attorney general and governor of Michigan has all of these attributes and is now a trenchant commentator on CNN. She broke Michigan's political glass ceiling for our current executive branch of state government comprised of a female governor, secretary of state and attorney general. I was very proud to have her support.

I first got to know her when she ran for attorney general in 1998. She resided in Southeast Michigan with her husband Dan Mulhern and three young children and had to navigate the state with all the silliness and unfair obstacles thrown in the way of female candidates (short hair is a must, she was instructed). Prior to Harvard Law School, she had done a stint in Hollywood, where the casting couch and other indignities raised her ire sufficiently to cause her to take on the good ol' boy world of law and politics.

In her first run for statewide office, Jennifer Granholm was a relatively unknown political figure in Southwest Michigan. I heard about her from Democratic Party friends and invited her to visit Kellogg Company. I/we were sold from the get go. She was a protean figure who could speak as a lawyer and a mother with a keen wit and commanding presence. She would go on to win the race against Republican John Smietanka, 52% - 48%.

In 2002, when term-limited incumbent Republican Governor John Engler was unable to run for re-election, Jennifer was a natural for the race and after securing the Democratic nomination in a three-way slugfest, she defeated the Republican Lieutenant Governor Dick Posthumus resoundingly 54% - 47%, knocking down another female political barrier. She was re-elected in 2006 defeating Dick DeVos, heir to the Amway fortune and husband of Betsy DeVos, current secretary of education for President Trump. Dick DeVos spent $35 million of his own money in a $42 million effort to unseat her, but he was no match for her grit and determination. She won handily, 56.3% to 42.3%.

I called Jennifer looking for an endorsement in early 2018, which she readily agreed to, but with the admonition that it would come with some baggage. Republicans had been attacking her years in office as the "lost decade," conveniently forgetting she had been governor while the national economy was collapsing under President George W. Bush. She was governor of Michigan, the heart of the car manufacturing industry, while the entire auto industry was teetering on bankruptcy and Mitt Romney was proposing to let them go under. The gall of the Republicans was astounding. It was Jennifer Granholm, working with newly elected President Obama, who kept the car companies from collapse and the state from entering a depression. The whole scene reminded me of the observation of Harold Nicholson, the famous British diplomat who cautioned,

"Once you reach the open sea, we forget how we clung to the pilot in the storm." She had been our pilot and had taken us through the heaviest of seas.

We snickered a bit when she warned me that the Republicans might run an ad with her face morphing into mine. Actually, an ad I would relish as someone grateful for her support.

Fast forward to late spring. I had received the endorsement of the Progressive Women's Alliance (PWA), which was a huge plus in a race with three other white males in a year that was becoming female centric. What if I could get Governor Granholm to headline a fundraiser for me in Michigan? No harm in asking, but realizing it was slim odds with her teaching at Berkeley, travel and CNN commitments. Well, so much for the odds. Turns out she was planning on being in Michigan on vacation over the 4th of July down around St. Joseph and generously agreed to interrupt her time off and participate in a lakeshore themed event on my behalf on Monday, July 2.

The entire campaign staff, especially Kathryn and A.J., went into crunch mode over this event. Not only did we have a former governor coming to help, but a national political figure and a trailblazer for women in politics in Michigan. Having her in state on my behalf would register with progressive women that she stood with me and also offered an opportunity to fill the coffers with some dollars for the final stretch.

We decided to hold the fundraiser at my home on Lake Michigan and Kathryn, doing her job, began to push to have a two-tiered event or a "clutch" as she liked to call it. A tiered event is where those who contribute more are invited to participate in a more intimate event with the guest of honor, in this case, Jennifer Granholm, before the general event. I always hated that arrangement when I attended fundraisers, but more importantly had committed to Annie months before in a wide ranging discussion of our principles that we would never do that. Despite the insistence of the staff and some good natured ribbing, I kept saying no. Finally, an exasperated Kathryn went to Eli, who wrapped it up telling her, "I don't know why he won't do it, but he isn't, so just drop it." I had committed to Annie and was not going to budge, but it was actually bigger than that. It is easy to see how in a campaign you can compromise on the edges, bend on your values and go down a path you never expected. This was a place to draw a line in the sand to prevent my own personal ethics creep.

It was a spectacular event due to the hard work of Kathryn, A.J., Heather and others. Pure Michigan is the title of the national promotional campaign for the state and the evening with Governor Granholm looked like a page out of that program. Perfect in every regard; weather, setting, tents, hors d'oeuvres and refreshments overlooking a blue, placid Lake Michigan and 130 or so attendees jacked up to see Jennifer Granholm. We decided to change what would be the normal batting order – introduction, guest, candidate – realizing the guests were looking forward to hearing from her, not me. Mark Schauer introduced me and I launched into my everyone wants a fair shot pitch and then introduced the governor. What a pro. She had ridden up with her husband Dan and with no briefing or prep seamlessly carried on where I left off. She wove in the notion of a fair shot, while espousing Democratic values and how my campaign encapsulated those attributes. Not only were her remarks spot on, but she was most generous with her time meeting with everyone; pictures, selfies as if she had no better place to be. A total class act.

If you run for political office, gird your loins. You will be attacked, whether warranted or not. The attacks on social media or negative advertisements on TV will occur because they work, especially in this day and age when you are guilty when accused. Forget the facts or even if the accuser hasn't a clue what they are talking about. In late spring and early summer of 2018, we got sliced and diced on two fronts, neither of which we had anticipated. The first involved a book I wrote in 2014 entitled, *Raisin Bran and Other Cereal Wars*, which was intended to be a realistic portrayal of life on Capitol Hill in the early 1970's and what I actually did as a lobbyist for Kellogg Company. Nothing theoretical, but reality.

Eponine Garrod and cohorts took exception to my description in the parlance of the era of the front office of former Congressman Charlie Wilson (D-TX) as not being respectful enough of women and portrayed me as some sort of misogynist. An interesting attack on someone who in the 1990's took on the sexual harassment policy at Western Michigan University as not being stringent enough (sexual harassment SHALL be cause for dismissal) and who had been endorsed by the most prominent female political trailblazer in Michigan. In addition, not only was the description apposite of the reality of the people and the period, it mirrored the description of many national publications and was the subject of a full blown Hollywood movie, *Charlie Wilson's War*, starring Tom Hanks. Maybe it just didn't fit Ms. Garrod's Potemkin Village image of what Capitol Hill should have been like in the 70's, but she spewed righteous indignation over social media.

What came next, was simply smarmy. On July 15, Rick and Mary Halpert hosted a fundraiser for me at the The Kalamazoo Park Club, which was well attended by a somewhat older crowd with the noticeable exception of two younger supposedly college students. I went up to talk with them and they confirmed, or maybe I should say claimed, that they were Kalamazoo College students. We had a brief chit-chat and I thanked them for coming. We all knew they were up to something and sure enough, they had come to surreptitiously record my answer when questioned about the so called offending paragraph in the book. Lee Atwater, the legendary Republican master of sleazy campaign tactics would have been proud of whoever put them up to it.

Now I don't know if someone recruited them or not, but I suspect so and if so what a sad commentary. I really thought we Democrats were better than that. I often said during the campaign that we don't beat the Tea Party by becoming the Tea Party. Likewise, we don't hold the moral high ground by using Nixon era campaign tactics. Ironically, they could have walked in with a recording device and put it on the table and I really wouldn't have given a damn. It is common knowledge that practically every utterance of a candidate is subject to public scrutiny, which is fine by me. What is not fine, is the implicit message in how it was done and if in fact they were college students recruited to replicate the modus operandi of campaigns devoid of morality made it all the more shameful.

Why stop at misogyny when you can allege tax fraud? Yep, tax fraud, by someone who could not possibly know the facts and if they did, obviously didn't know the law and based the whole outrageous claim on a sexist premise.

One afternoon while in the Glenn Post Office, Molly received a call from an unidentified Atlanta area code and upon answering was greeted by a clerk from the Fulton County Tax Assessor's Office. The clerk inquired as to whether this was Molly Franklin and was her husband running for Congress in Michigan. Molly responded, "Yes" and then inquired as to what this call was about. The clerk informed her that a woman from Michigan had called to ask whether our property in Atlanta was utilizing the homestead exemption (which it was, also called the PTE for property tax exemption) and then the "woman from Michigan" told the clerk that my previous residence in Kalamazoo had also claimed the homestead exemption. The clerk then responded to this Sherlock Holmes wannabe that such a situation was not permissible. After hearing out the clerk, Molly told her I would be giving her a call. I immediately called the clerk and informed her that our tax exemptions were totally legal and appropriate and that I would have our lawyer give her a call.

Meanwhile, as our lawyer pulls together the relevant information and statutes, Eponine Garrod puffed up like a proud peacock announcing that my wife and I are guilty of tax fraud. (Zachary Lassiter, whom I know only from Facebook, later raised an interesting angle, claiming that the Matt Longjohn campaign had approached David Benac about raising my tax issue and he had declined. I do not know if in fact that happened). The basis of her claim was so irresponsible that it could only be considered, at a minimum, an act of gross negligence or maybe she just lacked the gravitas of someone making such a claim. Only one person other than Molly and I who understood our tax status in Michigan and Georgia was our accountant. There was no way anyone but the three of us could know the factual basis behind our filings, but as Mark Twain was known to say, "Never let the truth get in the way of a good story."

Looking back on this whole sorry episode, I have come to appreciate how fundamentally sexist were the notions behind the charge. I am sorry Molly and I are not the Cleaver family of *Leave it to Beaver* living in a clapboard house with a white picket fence. Did it ever occur to Ms. Garrod and our accusers that getting married later in life after the death of my wife in our 50s might involve some non-traditional living arrangements? Did it ever occur to our accusers that my wife had created a product (which by the way helps thousands of people with special needs) and was CEO of a company she established in Atlanta, Georgia? Did they ever consider that she was a resident of Georgia, voted in Georgia and had never been domiciled in Michigan? Were they aware that we filed separate tax returns in Michigan and Georgia and as residents of two separate states qualified for the homestead exemption? It appears as if none of this was weighed in any fashion, but why bother with the facts or the law when you can score points with an unfounded charge for political gain.

Our lawyer in Georgia contacted the clerk and chastised her by emphasizing, "Her job was not to give legal advice" and that he would forward her the Georgia statute demonstrating our compliance with the law. I also contacted a Michigan tax lawyer who literally laughed when I told him the accusation was "tax fraud." Tax fraud generally requires the act to be willful and intentional, the so called mens rea, a mental state which is a very high standard to establish. He got a kick out of people throwing around terms they really don't understand. I found it less amusing, but was now impressed that my accusers were mind readers. Most importantly, he assured me there was no issue here.

In hindsight, this kerfuffle over our taxes does not have much import, but it is the apotheosis of the kind of specious attacks that sadly permeate our politics and discourage good people from running for office. Some people's conduct is simply petty like blocking my yard signs on both sides by the opponent.

*My yard sign blocked front and back by Matt Longjohn's signs.*
*Guess I should not feel so bad when people called him "short pants."*

All the while, I am getting castigated by fellow Democrats. The most gracious moment of the campaign was a result of a chance encounter with, of all people, Fred Upton's wife Amey. In mid-July, Molly and I went to a charity fundraising dinner in St. Joseph for Lory's Place, named for Dr. Lory Schults, a local podiatrist who died in a traffic accident. The organization helps children and families deal with grief. As we pulled up, standing alone outside was Amey Upton and as we walked up I thought to myself this will be interesting to say the least. After a couple of hello's, I went to shake her hand and she pulled back reflecting, "George, there are some things more important than politics," and proceeded to give me a hug. An extremely gracious act and a large lesson in humanness by a small gesture from a woman who is an ordained minister and leads the life she preaches.

Your interaction with people during a campaign will cause a range of emotions, and one such poignant moment has stuck with me. Interestingly, it did not have any relationship with a government policy or plan, but rather highlighted the limits of what government can do.

Annie and I attended a service at the First Presbyterian Church of Paw Paw led by a dynamic minister, the Reverend Tiffany McCafferty, a former practicing attorney and now someone seeking a higher calling. Following the service, we joined the congregation at a picnic in the local park with the usual fare of hot dogs, hamburgers, potato salad and the like served buffet style. After loading up some healthy portions, I grabbed a seat next to a diminutive older woman who while physically spritely seemed subdued. In conversation, I found out that she had recently moved to Paw Paw from Ohio to live with one of her children who I imagine determined it was time to look after mom, but when I asked how she was enjoying Paw Paw (a beautiful and welcoming town), she with sadness in her voice remarked how she missed her friends. I cannot know this with certainty, but it struck me how lonely she was and caused me on the drive home to ruminate on her and our obligation to take care of the elderly. My encounter with her impacted me in much the same way my meeting with the blue collar guy looking for work in the offices of the Special Subcommittee on Labor had struck a nerve in me years ago. It made me think what the hell are we all trying to accomplish? If you go to Congress you can fight for Medicare, Medicaid, Social Security, pension reform and all sorts of programs that help ensure senior citizens can live with dignity. There are, however, some aspects of the human experience which are beyond the scope of government. We should never quit trying, but whether you are a member of Congress, a U.S. senator, governor or even president; happiness, sadness or loneliness may be beyond the reach of those institutions. Regardless of whether it might be an exercise in futility, that elderly woman inspired me to keep charging ahead. She also re-imbued in me the belief that politics is about people, not power, and that you make decisions with your heart as well as your brain. Fundamentally, the issue should always be how do we make life a little better for everyone? Maybe there is no remedy for every ill, but that doesn't mean you should stop trying. As Mike Farrell, the actor of *MASH* fame is quoted as saying, "If you try to do your best, there is no failure." An attitude of mine reinforced on a Sunday in Paw Paw that also made running for Congress all the more purposeful.

Unlike some of the vexing issues affecting senior citizens, other elements impacting the quality of life and health sit foursquare with what government does and does not do. In the case of Otsego, government inaction ran into an indomitable young woman, who like the Parkland students, taught the adults a thing or two.

I met Mary Zack, founder of Justice for Otsego, when friends asked if I might volunteer some of my government relations expertise to her cause. Her story and the story of her community is both moving and compelling. Otsego is a tight knit town of approximately 4,000 residents about 20 minutes or so north of Kalamazoo in Allegan County. It had once been a prominent player in the paper industry with mills that dotted the region on the Kalamazoo River, but are now closed and abandoned. Mary had a typical small town upbringing where she attended Otsego High School (aptly named the Bulldogs when thinking of her), but this normality ended when she was diagnosed with ovarian cancer at age 17. Thinking it was essentially bad luck of the draw, she successfully fought it and moved on with her life. Years later, however, her sister was diagnosed with cancer at age 35 and it occurred to Mary that there seemed to be a disturbing and dispro-portional incidence of cancer among her former high school classmates. It was at this juncture, she became the Otesgo version of Erin Brockovich, forming Justice for Otsego, as a coalition for activism, to force state and federal government to investigate and remediate whatever adverse environmental factors were poisoning her town. Everyone knew the now defunct paper mills had for years dumped waste into the river and on farmland lying fallow. It turns out there was also a waste company that had been bringing in toxic materials from Kalamazoo and other industrial areas and dumping it willy-nilly in the vicinity of the river and abandoned farmland, now home sites, in violation of state and federal environmental laws. The nonfeasance of the government in the past was egregious and the casual connection between the environmental degradation and the incidence of cancer was glaring.

Since the 1990's, the Kalamazoo area had been listed on the Environmental Protection Agency (EPA) national priorities list, but the agency strapped for resources had to pick and choose where to allocate these limited resources. "It's really a matter of getting the government agencies activated and focused on this issue," I advised when speaking to the Otsego group. "It's real, it's significant and something needs to be done."

I had been asked to help and the lobbyist in me came out. How do we garner attention, get some action and fix the problem? My first call was to the lobbyist in Washington of the Environmental Defense Fund (Oh,

I forgot, lobbyist is a dirty word). They, like the EPA, are besieged with requests for help, but they were willing to contact Senator Stabenow's (D-MI) office with whom they had a relationship and see how they might help. My next call was to the senator's regional office in Grand Rapids.

There's a good reason Senator Debbie Stabenow keeps getting elected. She and her staff are both available and attentive. They care. As I was making the call, I was reminded how shortly after she had been elected in 2001, she made a visit to Battle Creek and I waggishly commented, "She had now been there more than her predecessor had been in the last six years." Mary Judnich, her regional director, did not disappoint us in Otsego. She was already aware of the controversy and agreed to join our working group for an update meeting in a local coffee shop. Prior to the meeting, she contacted the EPA and other appropriate agencies and in so doing, accomplished part of our mission. Her contact put the government agencies on notice that the senator was concerned and that they could rely on her support when they dedicated dollars and manpower to Otsego.

The calamity of Otsego and the responsiveness of Senator Stabenow and her staff is illustrative of what running for and holding public office should be all about. Making a difference in people's lives. Elected officials "lobby" on behalf of their constituents. Whether it is funding for roads, grants for a university or having a Superfund site cleaned up; they advocate within the government for the people who sent them there. In the case of Otsego, it is a complicated mess that is still being addressed. However, with the likes of Mary Zack, Mary Judnich and Senator Debbie Stabenow focused on results, I am confident that what is needed to be done will be.

The final days before an election turn the candidate into a modern day whirling dervish. Parades, picnics, house parties, fundraisers, community gatherings have you spinning from event to event. There is also an underlying sense of relief that this will be over soon. What seems like has gone on forever will have finality soon and it couldn't come quick enough.

*"It is fast approaching the point where I don't want to elect anyone stupid enough to want the job."*
**Erma Bombeck**

# Chapter 15

"It ends very abruptly. On August 7, 2018, not quite two years after the election of Donald Trump, I found out I would not be joining him in Washington, D.C.

Election Day was somewhat of a blurred surreal experience. I went to vote early that day at my polling place in Ganges Township, which is a modest town hall in front of a cornfield. The setting is very remote and rural, easily accessible with none of the lines associated with voting in an urban area. It is a strange sensation seeing your name on the ballot and checking the box. It caused me to pause for a moment and embrace what an adventure running for office entailed. Now all that work over a good year plus came down to a flick of the wrist as I voted for myself.

Leaving resulted in an election related activity we are all familiar with, but I had never experienced. Exit polling. Standing in front of the building was a man with a tablet. I was later told he was with *The New York Times* and was interviewing voters after they made their selections. He asked whether I voted Democratic or Republican and whether I was willing to participate. When I responded, "Democrat and yes," he proceeded to rattle off names of Democratic candidates for governor, attorney general, secretary of state, U.S. Senate until he got to the race for the U.S. House of Representatives and I was able to proudly announce I had picked George Franklin. I added an editorial comment by exclaiming that pick was a no brainer.

Somewhat counterintuitively, there is really not much for the candidate to do on Election Day since basically, as a candidate, in the words of Ricky Bragg the intuitive Southern author would say, "It is all over but the shouting." Now the candidate's staff is very busy with Get Out the Vote (GOTV), but your job at this juncture is to essentially stay out of their way. I think partly to keep me busy and out of the way, Eli and I attended a seniors' picnic after voting. The event was a pleasant distraction from ruminating over what was going on in hundreds of polling places in Southwest Michigan. It was heartening to have so many people tell you that they had seen my television ads and had voted for me. It is, however, a case of selective perception being buoyed by such comments since you don't factor in those folks who said nothing. Molly and I had decided to get a room in Kalamazoo to avoid a long drive home election night and not knowing how late an evening it might be before the results were conclusive. I brought two sets of clothes for the next day. One set was for if we were victorious, which meant I needed to be in Detroit by noon for the Democratic Party Unity lunch. The other set of clothes was for if we lost and we would go to the campaign headquarters to start cleaning up and clearing out. An activity, which conjured up in my mind the famous Norman Rockwell *Saturday Evening Post* cover of November 1958 entitled, "Elect Casey," or more appropriately referenced as "defeated candidate." It is a memorable scene in which an exhausted, dejected, disbelieving candidate finds out he has lost while "supporters" file out of the hall. Regardless of the outcome, win or lose, I was ready.

The polls closed at 8 p.m. and it would be a while after that before any real results came in, so Eli suggested, and it was a good one, that Molly and I stay away from the headquarters until some meaningful numbers were being posted. So that evening, we went to dinner with some dear friends, Dianne and Mike McCrann, took a few calls and generally made a low key evening of it. About 9 p.m., we went to join friends and campaign staff at the headquarters.

The early results and trends were not good and were consistent throughout the night. Matt Longjohn took an early lead, I was in second, David Benac third and Rich Eicholz fourth. Eli and I were in his office streaming the results on his laptop and hoping against hope that some area of the district would strongly break in my favor or that the absentee ballots would eliminate my steady deficit. Molly, as a veteran of numerous campaigns, knew better. When the staff and supporters start referring to absentee ballots as the salvation, you are probably toast. By 10 p.m. or so, reality set in. We knew, as Dandy Don Meredith of Monday night football would say, "The party was over," when the local TV news crew packed up to leave and go to the Matt Longjohn victory gathering. I had spent in round figures $800,000, made 12,991 fundraising calls, spent the equivalent of 16 forty-hour weeks in call time, attended hundreds of coffees, house parties, marches, rallies, fairs and gatherings while totally disrupting the lives of my wife and kids to come in second place, or as Dale Earnhardt would say, "First place loser."

I think Eli would still be staring at that computer, but shortly after 10 p.m. I said, "Let's call Matt Longjohn and congratulate him." Eli, always prepared, had the cell number of Matt Longjohn's campaign manager to whom we placed the call. Matt got on and I congratulated him on a hard fought campaign and he expressed his appreciation for the courtesy of the call. Professional on both sides. Now the hard part. It was gut wrenching to go out and announce to friends, volunteers and staff who had given it their all that I had called Matt Longjohn to concede. I did my best to thank them in words I am sure were insufficient to convey my gratitude and ended by imploring all to not quit on the process, stay involved and continue to make a difference. After some tears, hugs and gallows humor, we called it a night. I now had one thing in common with Abraham Lincoln, Bill Clinton, George W. Bush and Barack Obama. We all lost our first race for the House of Representatives.

——————— *Final Primary Election Results* ———————

### *Democratic Party Nominees*

| | |
|---|---|
| Matt Longjohn | 22,412 |
| George Franklin | 17,493 |
| David Benac | 12,867 |
| Rich Eicholz | 7,719 |
| **Total Votes** | 60,491 |

### *Republican Party Nominee*

| | |
|---|---|
| Fred Upton | 64,512 |

The Democratic primary turnout was up 300% from the past. Fred Upton, unopposed, tallied more votes than the entire Democratic field. The blue wave was real, but it would take Republican and independent votes for a Democrat to win.

According to my friend Sheila Smith, Matt Longjohn's campaign manager was quoted on Facebook at a fundraising event in Chicago as saying in regard to their race, "The speeches will be forgotten and the relationships will become distant memories and the only thing remembered, "Did you win?" I don't quite agree with the acerbity of that critique, but if you do well all I can say is that they didn't win. They came closer than anybody else, but that adds up to nothing.

I knew they had a problem in the fall during the general election when I ran into an acquaintance in the old Glenn hardware store and he asked me who I had lost to. When I told him Matt Longjohn, he responded, "Oh yeah, isn't he the guy who is running as a doctor who isn't really a doctor?" The Republican attack ads were taking a toll.

Unquestionably, Matt Longjohn is a doctor. He received a medical degree from Tulane University. The issue the Republicans raised, fair or not, was whether as someone who was not licensed to practice medicine was he misrepresenting himself as a physician. The distinction between someone with a medical degree, i.e. a doctor and someone licensed to practice medicine has a parallel in the legal world; the difference between a lawyer and an attorney. Being a lawyer does not mean you are an attorney and being an attorney does not mean you are a lawyer. Most people think they are one and the same, but not so. You are a lawyer when you graduate from law school and interestingly, in the context of this discussion, you are a "doctor" since your degree is a Juris Doctor. You can become an attorney without being a lawyer, just think power of attorney, which is often granted by banks. You are eligible to what we commonly think of practicing law when you pass the bar and become an attorney-at-law. (I passed the District of Columbia Bar and am still a member, albeit inactive since I no longer practice law). There is a difference between a lawyer and an attorney.

Likewise, in the medical world. When someone says they are a physician it conjures up an image of a Marcus Welby type practitioner healing the sick. If you are a physician, people assume that you are licensed. Matt Longjohn would often say, "As a physician" and is quoted in the press stating, "I'm a physician, an M.D. who is running for office to improve the health and quality of life for everyone in the district."

The whole brouhaha over what he was claiming or implying and the underlying suspicions on why he had not become a licensed physician permeated the political discourse during the general election. Former Congressman Joe Schwarz, who is a licensed medical doctor, may have categorized it best when he described the whole situation as "odd."

Now you can argue until the cows come home as to whether the Republican attack ads were fair or not, right or wrong, but regardless as to your opinion or as to the justice of the charges there can be little debate as to whether they were brutal and effective. The attack went to undermine the raison d'etre of his candidacy, which was health care and his medical qualifications that distinguished him from the incumbent. Both sides had super PACs weigh in on their behalf, but the one sponsored by the Congressional Leadership Fund maligning Matt Longjohn was exceptionally stinging, "Matt Longjohn is lying about his record. Longjohn isn't licensed to practice medicine, but he casts himself as a doctor, and that's not the only thing he is hiding." Tough, bare-knuckled politics.

One quite unexpected and significant blow to the Matt Longjohn campaign came from, of all people, Vice President Joe Biden, a few weeks before the November election. It actually was not something directed at Matt Longjohn, but rather effusive praise for Fred Upton coming from the former vice president of the administration who had putatively designated his opponent as one of "the top 100 innovators in health care in America." Coupled with the absence of any of the Obama leadership team campaigning for the Democrat nominee raised questions as to his prominence in the health care debate.

The setting was October 16 at Lake Michigan College in Benton Harbor, dead smack in the heart of the 6th Congressional District. Vice President Biden, went out of his way, to publicly proclaim that Fred Upton was, "One of the finest guys I have ever worked with." Technically not an endorsement, but the equivalent of one coming from the number two person in the Obama administration and arguably the leading contender for the Democratic nomination for president in 2020. As you can imagine, the Upton campaign pounced. Within days, an Upton for All of Us direct mail piece with the

Biden quote flooded mailboxes in the district. Now it is always difficult to gauge the impact of such a comment. I doubt it resulted in any Democrats flying the coop, but the acclaim from the likes of Joe Biden might have had an impact on independent and moderate Republicans who had considered it might be time for a change.

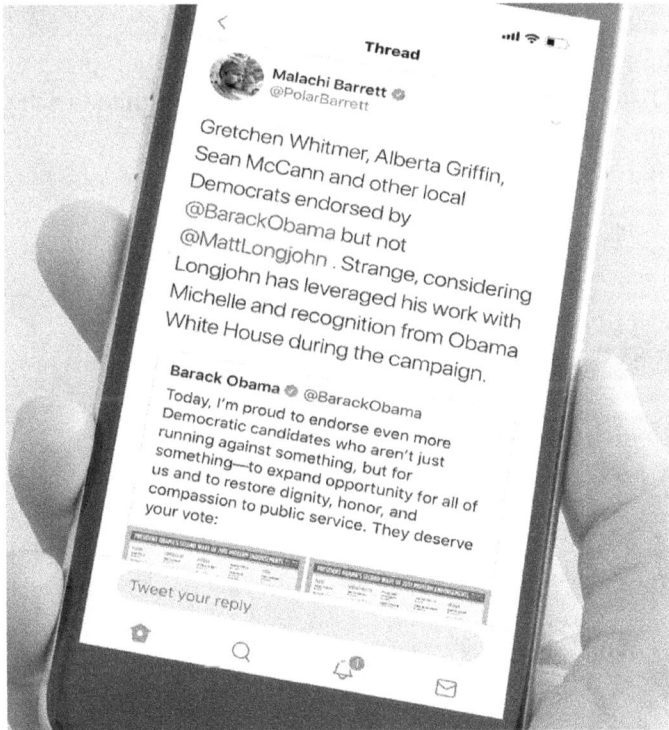

*Tweet by MLive reporter Malachi Barrett on Matt Longjohn not getting the Obama endorsement. Reverse of Sherlock Holmes. In politics, if the dog knows you, he barks!*

On November 6, 2018, the blue wave swept Michigan Democrats into power. Gretchen Whitmer was elected governor; Danna Nessel, attorney general; Jocelyn Benson, secretary of state and the Democrats picked up seats in the state Senate and state House of Representatives. U.S. Senator Debbie Stabenow was re-elected, and two seats in the U.S. House of Representatives flipped from red to blue with the victories of two impressive newcomers. Haley Stevens in the 11th District and Elissa Slotkin in the 8th District. The size of the wave was not enough to flip the 6th Congressional District. Fred Upton was re-elected to a 17th term.

——— *Final General Election Results* ———

### *Republican Party*
Fred Upton                         50.2%        147,436 Votes

### *Democratic Party*
Matt Longjohn                      45.7%        134,082 Votes

### *American Taxpayer Party*
Stephen Young                       4.1%         11,920 Votes

# Epilogue

Pursuant to Article I, Section 2 of the U.S. Constitution, on January 3, 2019, Democrat Nancy Pelosi was elected speaker of the House of Representatives by a vote of 220-192 over Republican Kevin McCarthy of California. She lost the support of 15 Democrats, three of whom voted "present" and 12 voted for someone else. The constitutional clause calling for the election of a speaker does not require (although all have been), the speaker to be a member of the House of Representatives, so vote recipients from the 12 defectors included some other members of the House, as well as former Vice President Joe Biden and former Georgia gubernatorial candidate Stacy Abrams. A check and balance on the Trump administration was now in place.

The 116th Congress is now in session and the number of individuals who could claim membership one time or another dating back to 1789 is 11,037 and with three vacancies to fill the total will be 11,040 by the end of 2019. The new Congress is a little different demographically than the previous 115th version, but really not dissimilar. Obviously, the biggest change is that in the House there are 235 Democrats vs. 197 Republicans (excluding the commissioner from Puerto Rico and four delegates) and, regardless how the elections for the vacancies play out, the Democrats will still be in control. The average age of 57.6 is slightly younger than the 57.8 of two years ago, but generally indistinguishable. The youngest member is Alexandria Ocasio-Cortez (D-NY) who is 29 and the oldest is Don Young (R-AK) at 85.

|  | *116th Congress* | | *115th Congress* | |
|---|---|---|---|---|
|  | **R** | **D** | **R** | **D** |
| Women | 13 | 89 | 23 | 64 |
| African American | 1 | 52 | 2 | 45 |
| Hispanic/Latino | 7 | 35 | 10 | 29 |
| Asian American | 1 | 16 | 1 | 14 |
| Native American | 4 | 4 | 2 | 0 |

The House of the 116th is, like past Congresses, overwhelmingly Protestant and Catholic:

| | |
|---|---|
| 233 or 53.5% | Protestant |
| 141 or 32.4% | Catholic |
| 26 or 5.9% | Jewish |
| 6 | Mormon |
| 3 | Muslim |
| 3 | Hindu |
| 2 | Buddhist |

Other religious affiliations represented include Pentecostal Christian, Unitarian Universalist, Greek Orthodox, and Seventh-Day Adventist.

In the post-mortem of the campaign, I fielded a lot of questions and observations, many of which I found to be generally shared by others who experienced running for office. The commonality of undertaking a run for political office hit home when I attended a national conference at the Massachusetts Institute of Technology (MIT) in Boston on January 12, 2019. The event was for Democratic congressional candidates (Republican event upcoming) to compare notes on all aspects of being a candidate for Congress. I dubbed it the losers conference since the 30 or so of us former candidates in attendance would have been in Washington if we had won. It was generally interesting and informative. It also confirmed that what I felt and endured was consistently shared by others. Yes, call time is "soul sucking" and you better have "alligator skin." I highly recommend attending this conference in the future to anyone considering entering the political fray.

The toughness of your skin aspect raises the ancillary issue of why don't people sue for defamation of character when wild unsubstantiated accusations are made against them. In a nutshell, because you can't win. You give up a lot when you run for office, but you also acquire the epithet "public figure." A designation, which encumbers you legally, unlike your neighbors, under the Supreme Court case of *The New York Times* vs. Sullivan in 1964. Per the Sullivan case, in order for a public figure to prevail in a libel (written) or slander (spoken) lawsuit as a public figure, you need to prove actual malice which in turn requires the perpetrator to have acted knowingly or with reckless disregard for the truth. A standard very hard to establish that allows your attacker, in essence, to use their ignorance as a defense. It always struck me as a hell of a note that ignorance should work to someone's advantage under the law, but that is the way it is.

I am becoming more convinced than ever that divided government is healthy and the situation we are now in with President Trump reinforces that notion. Six of President Trump's inner circle, including his campaign manager, deputy campaign manager, national security adviser and personal lawyer have been charged with felonies, and five of the six have pleaded guilty or convicted. Three of his Cabinet members, Tom Price of Health and Human Services, Ryan Zinke of Interior and Scott Pruitt of EPA have resigned under the cloud of an ethics violation as has Brenda Fitgerald the Head of the Center for Disease Control (CDC). The U.S. Attorney for the Southern District of New York (SDNY), Geoffrey Berman, a Republican appointee, has President Trump, his personal attorney and the Trump campaign under investigation for campaign violations relating to hush money being paid to two porn stars. They also have the Trump Inaugural Committee under investigation for trading favors for contributions. If ever congressional oversight was needed, it is now.

Donald Trump was the impetus for my running for office, and his conduct over the past two years has justified my decision. Whether or not you agree with his policies, his personal conduct is often vile and a disgrace to the office. Thank God my father, a World War II vet, never had to experience him in office and his treatment of former Senator John McCain. Here is a draft dodger who evaded service in Vietnam by fraudulently creating medical records indicating he had bone spurs denigrating a national hero just months after his death. His ignoble comments directed at the senator and his service were beyond the pale of decency. It is indicative of his character or lack thereof are his attacks on President Obama of on all things, golf. A discussion of golf and the president should be a petty distraction, not worthy of comment, but with Trump it pretty well sums up the man. In August of 2016, after castigating President Obama for years for playing too much golf, candidate Donald Trump harrumphed, "I'm going to be working for you. I'm not going to have time to play golf." A statement that has proven to be, in common parlance, total BS. Since being elected, in his first year, Trump played approximately 75 rounds of golf as opposed to President Obama who played 31 rounds in the first year of his administration. In the second year of their administrations, President Trump clocked in 63 rounds vs. President Obama's 27. He now has a two-year average that has him exceeding President Obama by 138%. As far as golf is concerned, according to the *Huffington Post* as of May 20, 2019, "Donald Trump's golf habit has already cost taxpayers at least $102 million in extra travel and security expenses," not to mention the installation of a $50,000 golf simulator in Trump's White House. The man simply has no shame.

It is said you can determine the mettle and the character of a person by their conduct on a golf course. In the case of Donald Trump, his comport on the course is not a pretty picture. According to many accounts, he flat out cheats. As LPGA pro Suzann Petterson put it, "He most likely pays his caddy well because every time he found his ball it was in the fairway." His conduct is so flagrant that *Sports Illustrated* writer Rick Reilly has penned a book entitled, *Commander in Cheat: How Golf Explains Trump*. The spillover into his administration is so egregious that the ever stalwart Republican newsletter, *The Wall Street Journal*, has editorialized on his administration mendacity as, "A core problem with Mr. Trump's governance: His frequent and almost casual dishonesty."

Except for rare occasions, as with *The Wall Street Journal* cited above, the conservative press shrugs off the character issues which, for some reason, loomed large with the Clintons. Likewise, with the amount of golf played – the subject of much consternation when Obama was president. The $3-4 million cost of each weekend trip to Mar-a-Lago now are not worthy of attention. I guess porn stars, draft dodging, alternative facts and a trillion dollar a year deficit are nothing to be concerned about by the Republican base. Maybe the new symbol for the GOP, instead of the elephant, should be Alfred E. Neuman of *MAD Magazine* accompanied by his slogan, "What, me worry?"

President Trump's conduct and character in office has, in retrospect, validated my initial thoughts after his election. Now, however, a few months after the general election of 2018, three questions keep coming up. Would I do it over? Could I have won? Am I glad I am not there now (meaning in Congress)?

As far as would I do it over, I waver in my answer which I guess means I am not sure. It was a once in a lifetime exhilarating experience that afforded me the opportunity to meet a lot of wonderful people. It was also a grueling process with your opponents and detractors trying to capture that gotcha moment. Raising money is God awful. I had heard that from every political figure, right or left, Democrat or Republican I have ever known, but experiencing it first hand was another matter. I don't agree when I hear other candidates describe it as demeaning since that is a word that connotes below one's status. Candidates are citizens applying for a job and their fellow citizens are doing the hiring. Incumbents and non-incumbents have no different status than any other citizens. It seems like all this money being raised and spent in political campaigns is such a waste. Wouldn't it be time better spent learning about issues and solutions in a blighted neighborhood rather than call time? I remember towards the end of the campaign before another forum commenting to David Benac something to the effect that I know you don't like me very much, but I want you to know that I have a great deal of respect for you. I imagine he was somewhat taken back by that statement, but I did and do still have respect for him. He was/is honestly trying to change the system from what he aptly called an auction to a system less dependent on money. I agree with him on the objective, I just don't know how to accomplish it as a practical matter. Campaign finance becomes a sticky wicket when you get to specifics. I was on Capitol Hill when the Federal Election Campaign Act was written and the issues we grapple with now are the same as back then. If you have matching funds, who qualifies? Do spending limits benefit incumbents? Is curtailing issue advocacy unjustifiably limiting free speech? When does issue advocacy become candidate promotion? It goes on and on. I am not saying because it is difficult we should not try, but it is not simple by any means.

Could I have won the general election is an unanswerable question. The only thing we "know" is that the Democratic nominee did not win. Our campaign lost the primary because of me – the candidate. We had a great campaign team with adequate resources, but for a variety of reasons not enough people liked me enough (or flat out disliked me) or didn't think I could win or do the job to vote for me. The corporate/small business background that came with a centrist aura was not going to fly in a Democratic primary. The lobbyist career and my support for Republicans, we knew from the get go, was going to be an albatross around my neck. Age factored in as a modest negative and being the establishment candidate (Blanchard, Levin, Granholm, Schauer) had some downside in an election where a lot of voters were looking for something new. Ironically, the aforementioned negatives in a Democratic primary might have been positives in a general election. As I often said, "I was a corporate officer of Kellogg Company and have had my own small business for 12 years. What are they going to do, call me anti-business?" The reality is that I probably would not have won in November, however, one tactical approach we had might have made the difference.

Fred Upton is a very popular and likeable guy, and the Democratic nominee made the mistake of running against him. I am not being facetious. I was and would have run against Donald Trump. He was the reason I was running and he was the issue. I never mentioned Fred Upton in my TV ads, my direct mail or other literature. There were references now and then to Fred Upton, but the focus was President Trump and how to hold him accountable in Congress for who he was and what he stood for. My campaign was going to be a referendum on the character and presidency of Donald J. Trump.

The final question I hear to this day, and one I get a kick out of is, "Aren't you glad you are not there?" The answer is no. I wish I had won. Often times the question is really just a nice way of making you feel better after losing. It reminds me of Bob Dole when asked how he felt after losing the election for president, he responded, "He went home and slept like a baby. He woke up every couple of hours and cried."

I wasn't going to stay very long if I won – two or three terms – which is something I think would have been a positive in the general election with Republicans and Democrats. It also would have been liberating as a member of Congress to be not so worried about the next election. I would have been in that enviable position of being able to just do "what is right," realizing that the definition of that term depends on each citizen's position. I would have compromised on many issues, refused to budge on some, while doing what I believed was correct without much concern for the political consequences.

To all the armchair quarterbacks out there, I suggest you give the candidates and elected officials a break. Sure they were not forced to run or serve, but thankfully they did. Most people involved in politics, elected officials, candidates, party workers, staff and volunteers are there for all the right reasons. We need to keep good people involved and to do so, we need to eliminate the viciousness now present in the political process and maintain civility and respect. If we fail in this regard, the only losers will be us the voters.

# *Acknowledgements*

My parents taught me you can never say thank you enough, and in this case, it is hard to know where to begin and where to end.

Why don't we start with the voters of the 6th Congressional District of Michigan, both Republicans and Democrats, who were most gracious and welcoming. It meant a lot when total strangers, and not necessarily ones supporting me, would come up and say, "Thank you for doing this."

To all the volunteers and contributors who invested time and treasure, no words of appreciation will ever suffice. All I can say is I gave it my all.

I am forever grateful to a campaign staff who did everything the right way and with a better candidate could have beaten anybody anywhere.

Thanks to the countless friends and family who stepped up to support me and especially my two daughters who wcrc always encouraging and "starred" in my TV ads.

Then there is the love of my life, my wife Molly, who allowed our lives to be totally disrupted while soldiering through parades and petitions – always smiling and supportive.

Finally, there is that guy who walked into the Special Subcommittee on Labor looking for a job when I was a congressional "go-fer." I will never know who he was, but he taught me all about what it is to want a fair shot and I am forever indebted.

# About George

George Franklin has worn a lot of hats in his career.
Lawyer, Lobbyist, Businessman, Candidate,
Author, Speaker…

Author of the acclaimed book on corporate lobbying,
*Raisin Bran and Other Cereal Wars,*
Franklin was a Democratic candidate for Michigan's
6th Congressional District in 2018. While, he lost the
primary, he survived to write about it
with humor and insight in his latest tell-all book,
*So You Think You Want to Run for Congress.*

*© George Franklin | GeorgeFranklinAuthor.com*